LIGHT THROUGH THE TREES

LIGHT THROUGH THE TREES

PHOTOGRAPHS AT **THE MORTON ARBORETUM**

PETER J. VAGT

3 FIELDS BOOKS
An imprint of the University of Illinois Press

Manufactured in China
C 5 4 3 2 1
♾ This book is printed on acid-free paper.

Library of Congress Cataloging-in-Publication DataNames: Vagt, Peter J., author.
Title: Light through the trees: photographs at the Morton Arboretum / Peter J. Vagt.
Description: [Urbana, Illinois]: 3 Fields Books, an imprint of the University of Illinois Press, [2022]
Identifiers: LCCN 2021045192 (print) | LCCN 2021045193 (ebook) | ISBN 9780252044601 (cloth: acid-free paper) | ISBN 9780252053610 (ebook)
Subjects: LCSH: Photography of trees–Illinois. | Landscape photography–Illinois. | Morton Arboretum–Pictorial works.
Classification: LCC TR726.T7 V34 2022 (print) | LCC TR726.T7 (ebook) | DDC 779/.3609773–dc23
LC record available at https://lccn.loc.gov/2021045192
LC ebook record available at https://lccn.loc.gov/2021045193

Dedicated to all at The Morton Arboretum
who work, serve, volunteer, and contribute,
and to the generations before them who did the same,
to make it the place where I—and millions—love to go to see trees.

CONTENTS

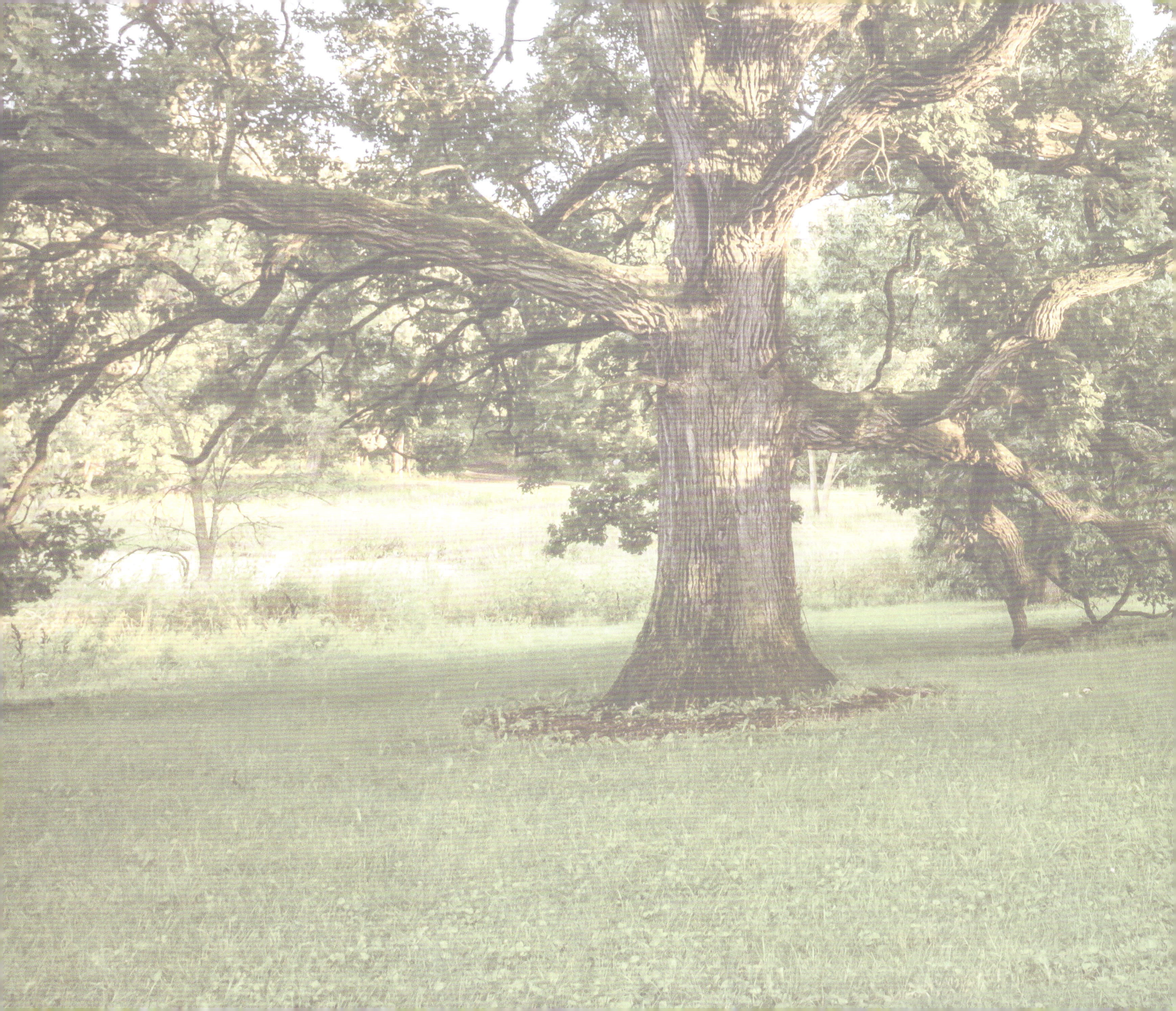

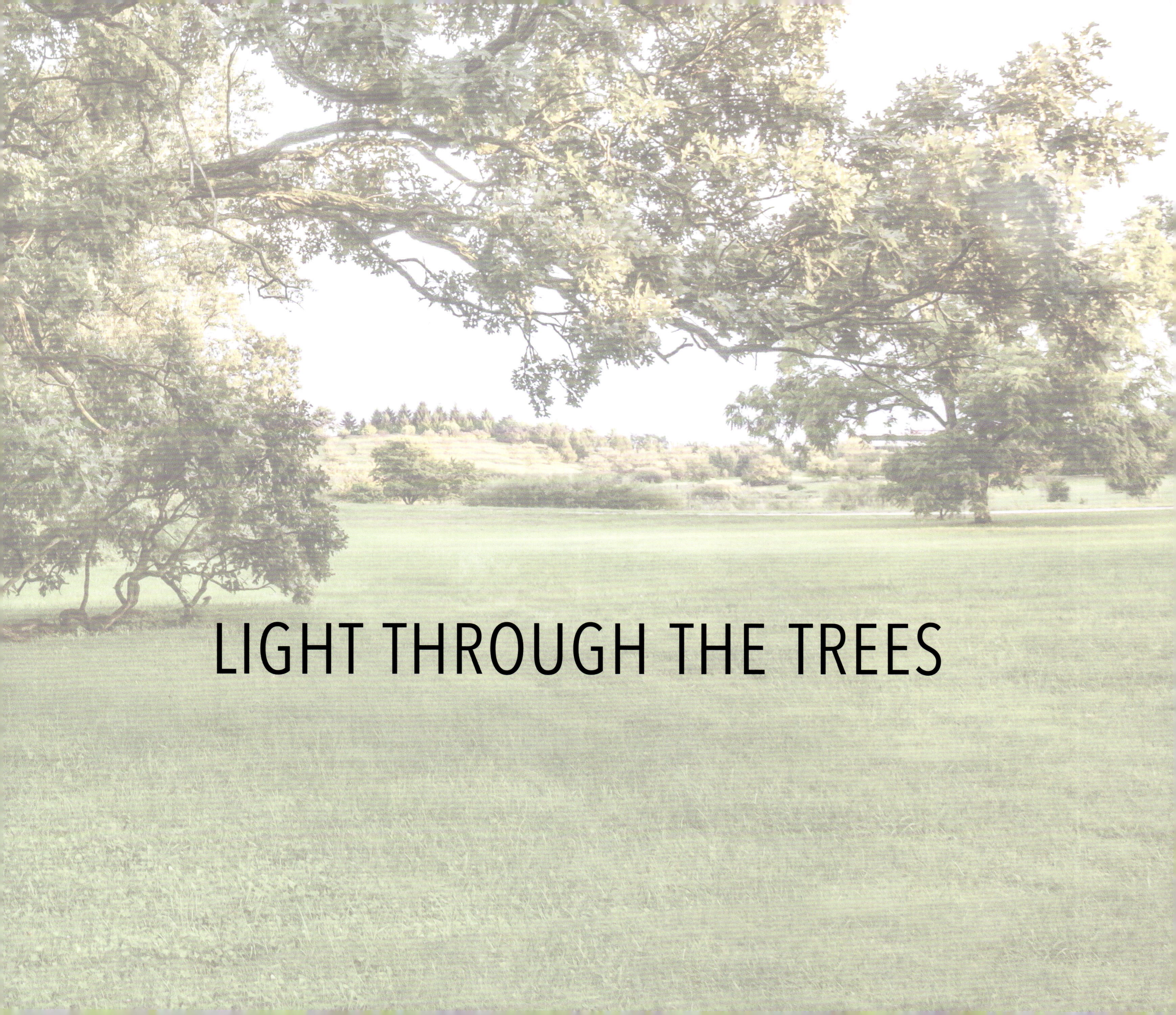

LIGHT THROUGH THE TREES

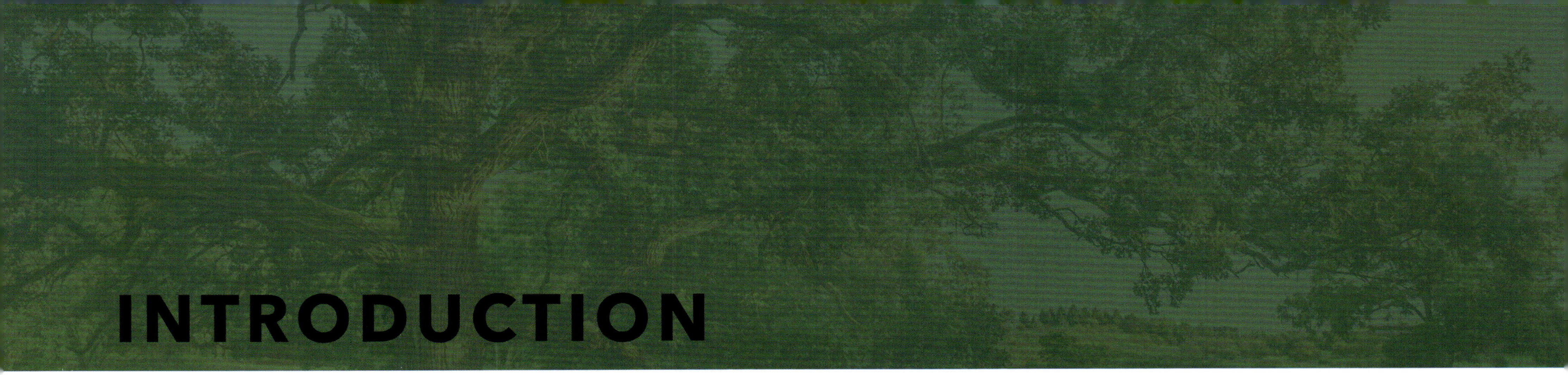

INTRODUCTION

Trees are beautiful. Individual trees, two or three trees together, and groups of trees in their communities of nature—anywhere we find them, trees are beautiful. Their graceful forms, the texture of their bark, their delicate leaves, the way they reach toward each other and toward the sky, their guardian-like presence over everything around them, and the changing patterns they make in sunlight throughout the year, all these things attract us to trees. We love to look at them, admire them, enjoy them, and be among them. And the best place to do that is near where we live.

Growing up on a Minnesota farm, trees were our mountains. Nothing was taller. Trees introduced me to new perspectives; climbing our linden tree, I could see over the roof of our house and across miles of corn growing in all directions. Scattered around in those miles of corn, I saw occasional groups of trees that farm families like ours had planted to protect their homes and barns from fierce westerly winds. At age eleven, I began to explore my surroundings with a camera. While walking with black-and-white film in my Kodak Hawkeye box camera, my first favorite subjects to photograph were trees and their shadows in snow and branches covered with frost.

As a college student transplanted to the energetic Chicago area, I was desperate to find open spaces with trees to look at and walk among. The Morton Arboretum was soon a refuge. Later, living and working in the Chicago area, this sanctuary of trees became my go-to place to walk and feel revived. It became my studio, my place to do art.

Influenced by Eliot Porter and Paul Caponigro, I realized that photography can do more than document subjects and scenes—even ones with beautiful trees. Like other media, photographs become art when they transcend the subject and reveal to us what it feels like to see that subject, person, or scene. When the experience of seeing the photograph transforms us, such a photograph has crossed the great chasm from being a pretty picture to being art.

My habit is to go to particular places at The Morton Arboretum again and again, in all seasons and all weather. I go early and late, on sunny and cloudy days, foggy and rainy days, and I go when snow is falling. I look for a new light to reveal something in these stands of trees, in their shadows, reflections, and surroundings that I've not seen before.

I've taken thousands of photographs here. The eighty-four photographs in this book are the ones that, for me, transcend what these trees, and the nature around them, look like. These are the photographs I was trying for throughout many years. These are the photographs that show me what it feels like to be here—what it feels like to see these trees and their settings. These photographs show me why I come away changed and renewed in the midst of daily life when I take the time to walk among trees.

In this book, I offer my portrait of trees and the nature surrounding them at The Morton Arboretum, and I offer a description of the way I take pictures. Organized generally throughout the seasons of the year, I hope these photographs inspire—especially my co-Midwesterners—not to wait for a trip to the Rockies or Yosemite to experience nature, but to get out and walk locally, in everyday life, to see and enjoy trees where we find them. If, like me, you bring a camera with you, I'm sure you'll stay even longer seeing and enjoying the trees that live near you. On some days, you'll find peace and balance in your life just from seeing and enjoying the trees where you live. Take a look inside this book, take a walk outdoors, see more trees, take more pictures of them, and see your life change.

The Morton Arboretum

The Morton Arboretum is a 1,700-acre public garden serving the Chicago area and the world as a champion of trees. I join over one million visitors to The Morton Arboretum each year in seeing and enjoying the trees. Here, I regularly walk sections of the sixteen miles of trails through The Morton Arboretum's woodlands and around its lakes, ponds, and wetland areas, stopping to see and focus on my favorite trees. This beautifully cared-for and much-loved tree museum invites us to walk, hike, study, and enjoy a variety of nature-focused education, recreation, and nature-arts opportunities.

How did this beautiful "tree museum" come about? Joy Morton, the founder of Chicago-based Morton Salt Company, established The Morton Arboretum in 1922 at his residence and to become a museum of trees. In 1872, his father, J. Sterling Morton, originated Arbor Day. As a legacy of the family's motto "Plant Trees," more than 4,200 tree species reside at The Morton Arboretum, which serves not only the region but the world as a credentialed museum and scientific tree science research and professional training center.

The Project that Led to the Book

Twenty-two years ago, while vacationing in Maine, I noticed beautiful photographs with fresh interpretations of iconic scenes of the region hanging in shops and galleries. Clearly there were talented photographers in the area who loved the coast of Maine. I admired their work and their ability to distill their feelings about what they saw into their pictures.

Back from vacation and back at work, my regular escape from hectic city life was spending time at The Morton Arboretum. As a serious photographer myself, and inspired by these Maine artists, I set out to create a portfolio of beautiful photographs to reflect my own love for walking at the Arboretum. I started going to the Arboretum several times a week at different times of day, seeking special trees and groupings, watching for changes in light, and waiting to find pictures that show what it felt like to be there.

Immediately and remarkably, within weeks of my return from Maine, I took the first picture of my portfolio, *Cathedral Pines* (Plate 10). I'm grateful to the Arboretum Store for featuring this photograph, and many that followed, and to the public who have made *Cathedral Pines* my most successful and beloved picture to date.

Over the next twenty years, I immersed myself in the woods and glades of the Arboretum every chance I got. From Walden (Henry David Thoreau, 1854) to Biophilia (Edward O. Wilson, 1984), to The Nature Principle: Reconnecting with Life in a Virtual Age (Richard Louv, 2012), and writings in between, I found resonance and encouragement about the restorative power of time spent in nature and the value of making nature experiences a part of every day.

While I walk, I look for pictures that show the essence of a location, that show why I feel restored just by looking at, and being near, a particular tree, or two or three. When I succeed, I add the photograph to my portfolio. My portfolio has grown, sometimes by just one new photograph a year, sometimes by four or five a year, occasionally by a few more.

Three years ago, I began to work on a book of my best photographs, hoping to inspire others to spend more time experiencing nature where they live. Believing that looking for pictures can also extend one's time in nature, I also wanted to include my method for finding rather than taking pictures. My method is not to follow rules of composition but to respond to the light, color, design, and life in nature I see in front of me and allow my feelings to guide me and distill what I'm seeing and feeling into a picture.

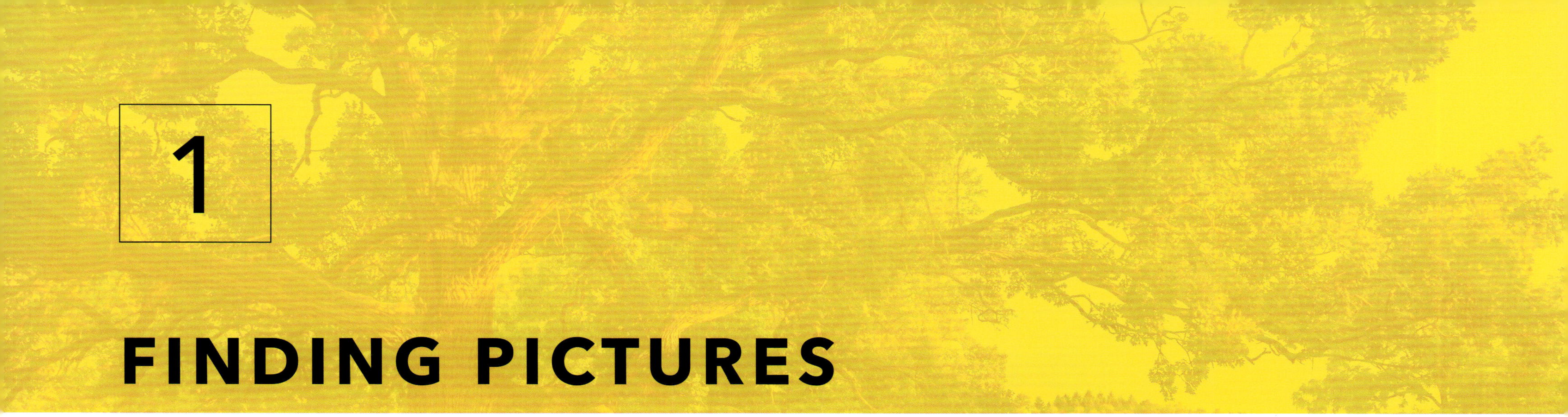

1

FINDING PICTURES

My habit is to go to particular places again and again, in all seasons, all weather, and at all times of day, looking for just the right light to reveal something I've not seen before in these stands of trees and along these trails. Being surrounded by nature allows me to breathe more deeply, and seeing my favorite trees in ever-changing light makes my mind stop clanging with stress. Calm seeps into me and I begin to feel what I'm seeing.

When I start to feel that wonderful sense of soothing calm, I know there's a possibility of finding a picture. *Find* is the key word. I don't compose pictures; I find them in the colors, patterns, and shadows of the trees in front of me. While I walk, I let my feelings well up in my consciousness. My feelings guide me to find what I'm seeing and feeling and distill it into a picture.

Sometimes I'm tempted to start clicking my camera at every interesting thing I see. But when I click too quickly, I can move on too soon and may miss a picture that has that distillation. If I keep looking, keep taking it in, I'm more likely to find a picture that transcends what the trees look like, and find one, instead, that shows what it feels like to be there seeing these trees on this day at this time—a picture that may even reveal something about life itself.

How do I (how does anyone?) know when, or if, I've found such a picture? My tests: Does the picture draw me in? Do I enjoy looking at it again and again? Do I never tire of looking at it? Do I feel I'm going somewhere inside this picture—into a world that extends beyond it? If I look at the middle, and then my eyes travel to every corner, and then all the way around the picture, are my eyes eager to start again? In other words, does it feel as though there's a circular song in this picture that I enjoy listening to? Does the picture feel complete? Pictures with a string of "yeses" are the "keepers." They join my portfolio. They are the pictures in this book.

2

FINDING PICTURES IN SPRING

Timing Matters

During two glorious weeks in April, the Arboretum *is* daffodils. At first, hundreds and then thousands of daffodils fill glades and line the roadways throughout the grounds. In 1999 when I began this project, and every year since, I've spent multiple April days here photographing daffodils.

But it wasn't until April 2002 that I found *Daffodil Glade* (Plate 1). On my lunch break with the sun overhead (usually not the best conditions for photography), light clouds muted the potential for harsh noontime shadows, and the breezes had stilled. I left the path and walked past many daffodils to the east end of the glade. I turned, looked back, and saw wave after wave of yellow flowers extending to the tree line at the other end of the glade. Massive, unmoving tree trunks provided a horizontal balance to the delicate, bright, bobbing daffodil blossoms. Now, years later, looking at this picture still brings me the joy of walking in April among these first flowers.

Timing matters. Spring bulbs and flowering trees bloom at varying times from year to year, which creates a varied annual palette. After many years of scouting the spring lakeshore, on a May 2009 evening walk, in the setting sun, I was startled to see six clumps of late-blooming daffodils alongside an electric blue blaze of bluebells. I had found *Daffodils and Bluebells* (Plate 3).

1. *Daffodil Glade*, West Side, 2002

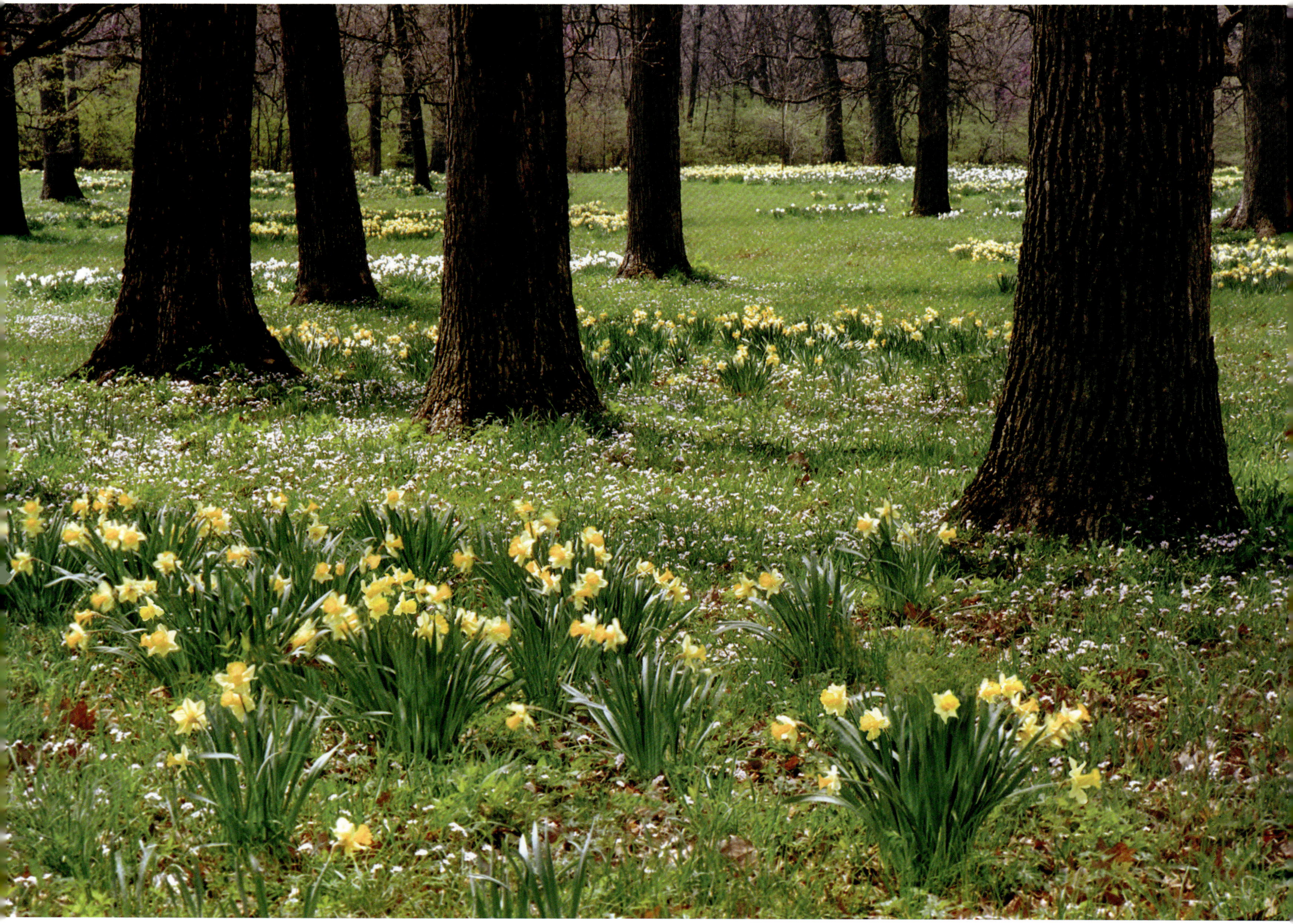

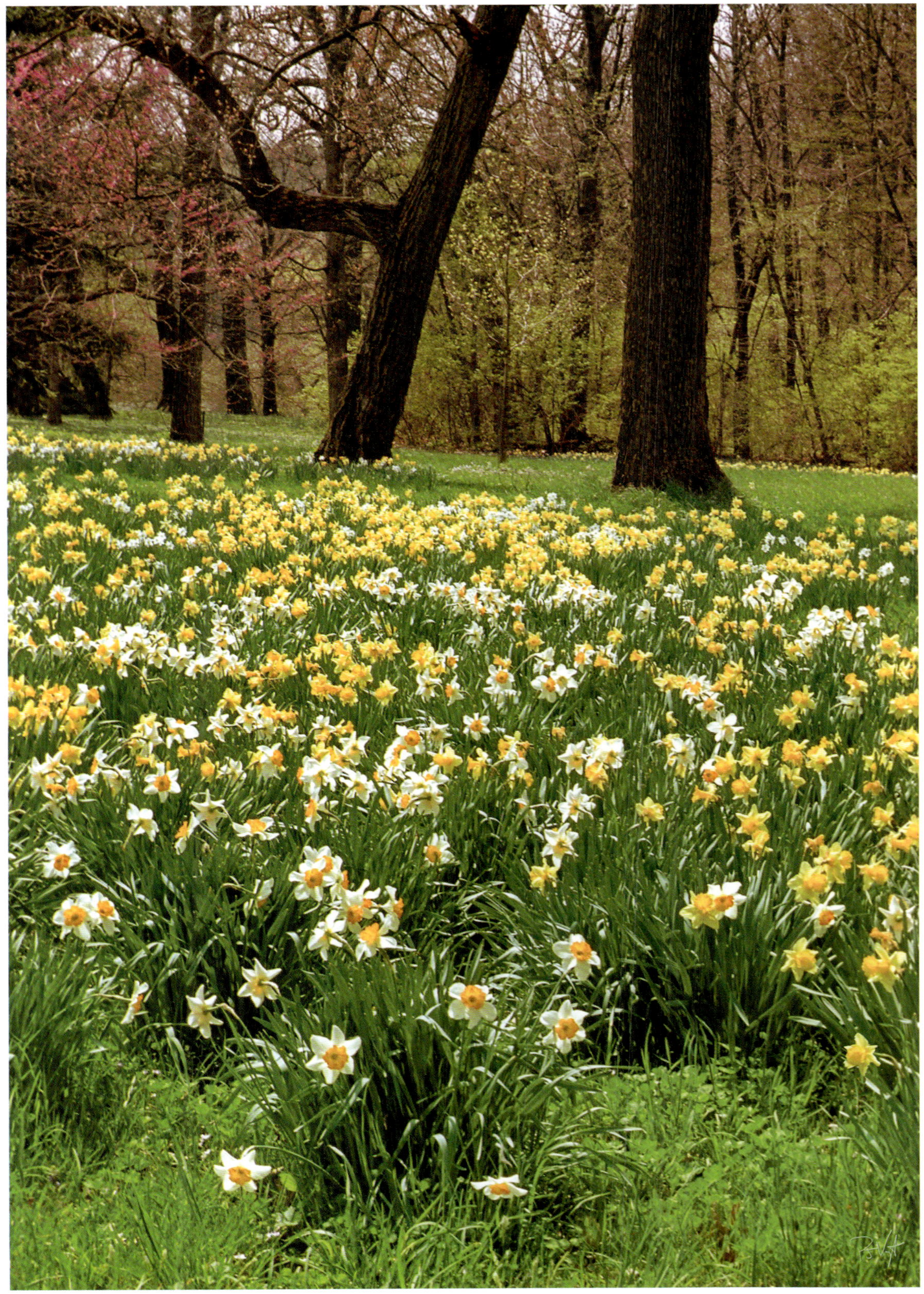

2. *Daffodils and Redbud Tree*, near Parking Area P26, 2002

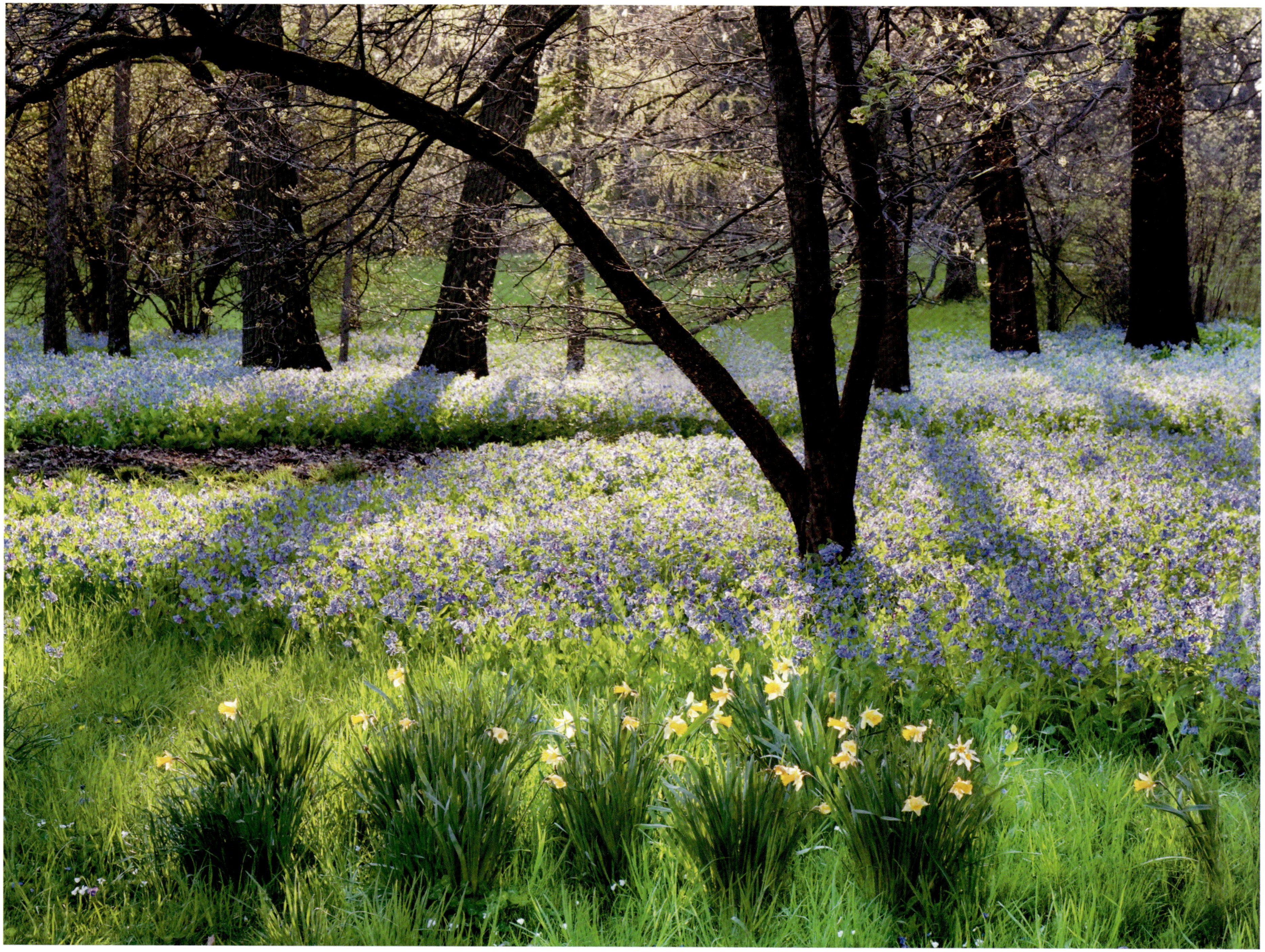

3. *Daffodils and Bluebells*, near Lake Marmo, 2009

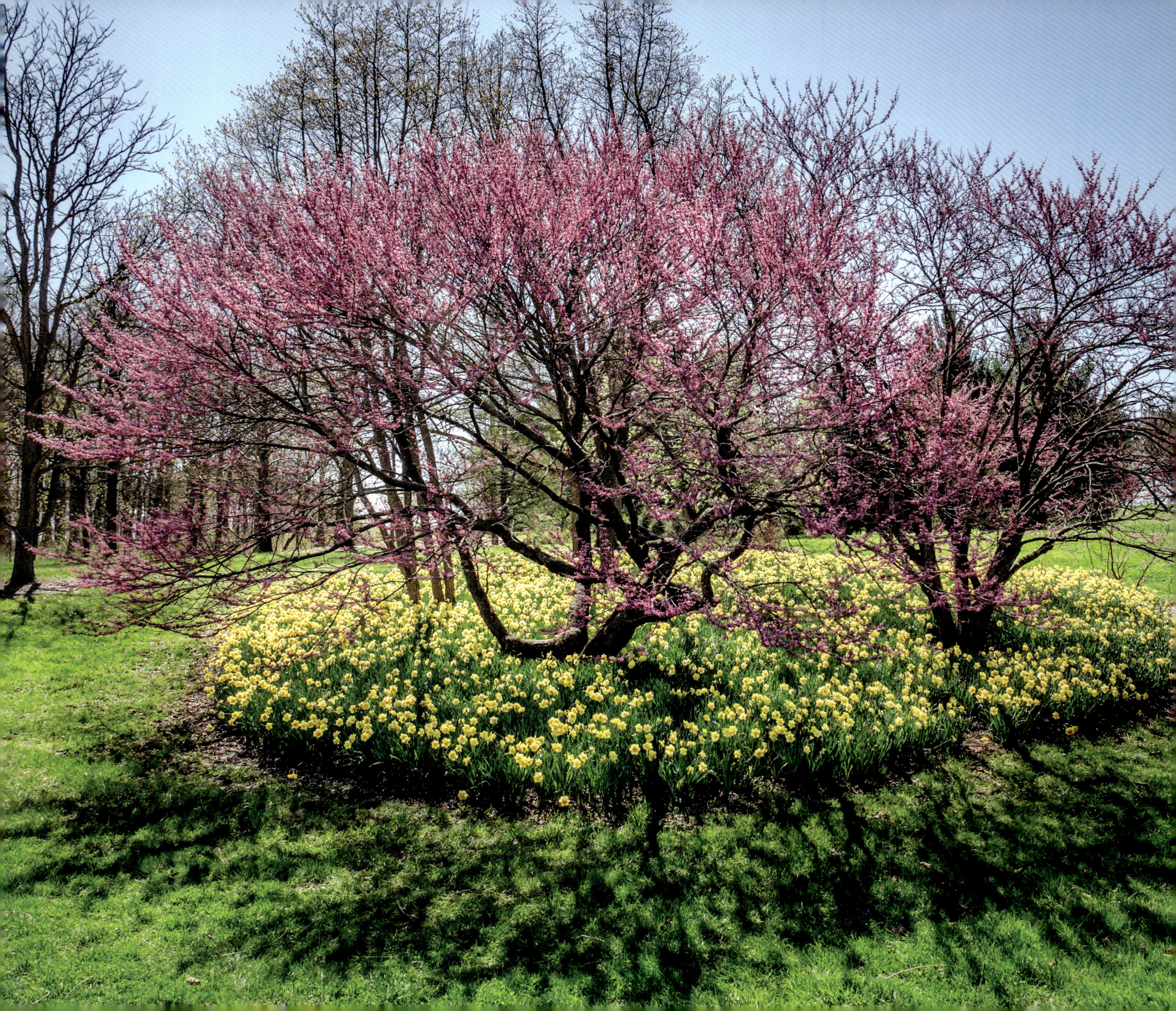

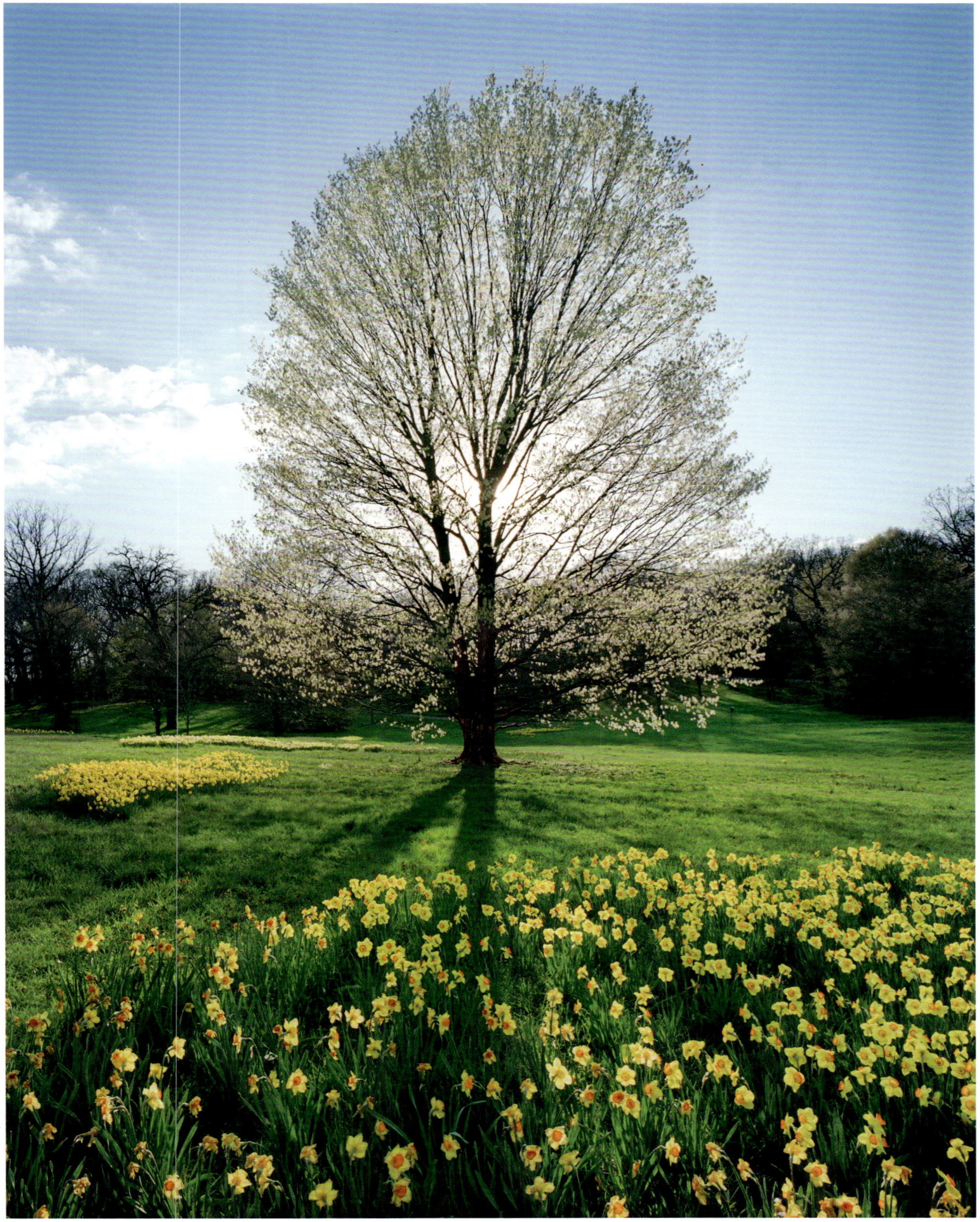

4. *Daffodils Circling Redbud Trees*, near Parking Area P2, 2017 (opposite)
5. *Maple Tree with Daffodils*, near Parking Area P14, 2006

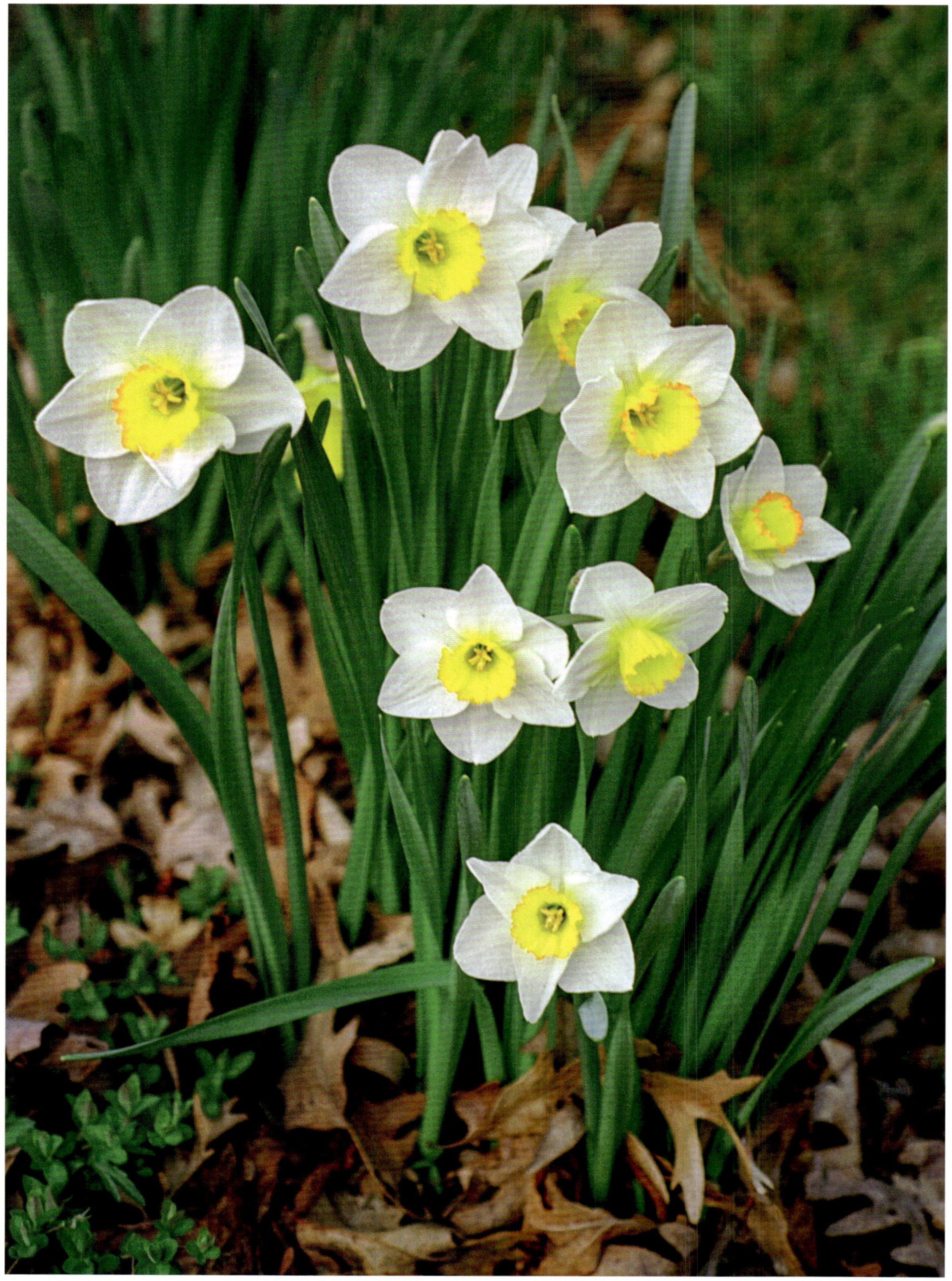

6. *Narcissus Bunch up through Oak Leaves*,
Daffodil Glade, 2000
7. *Four Daffodils*, Daffodil Glade, West Side, 2006 (opposite)

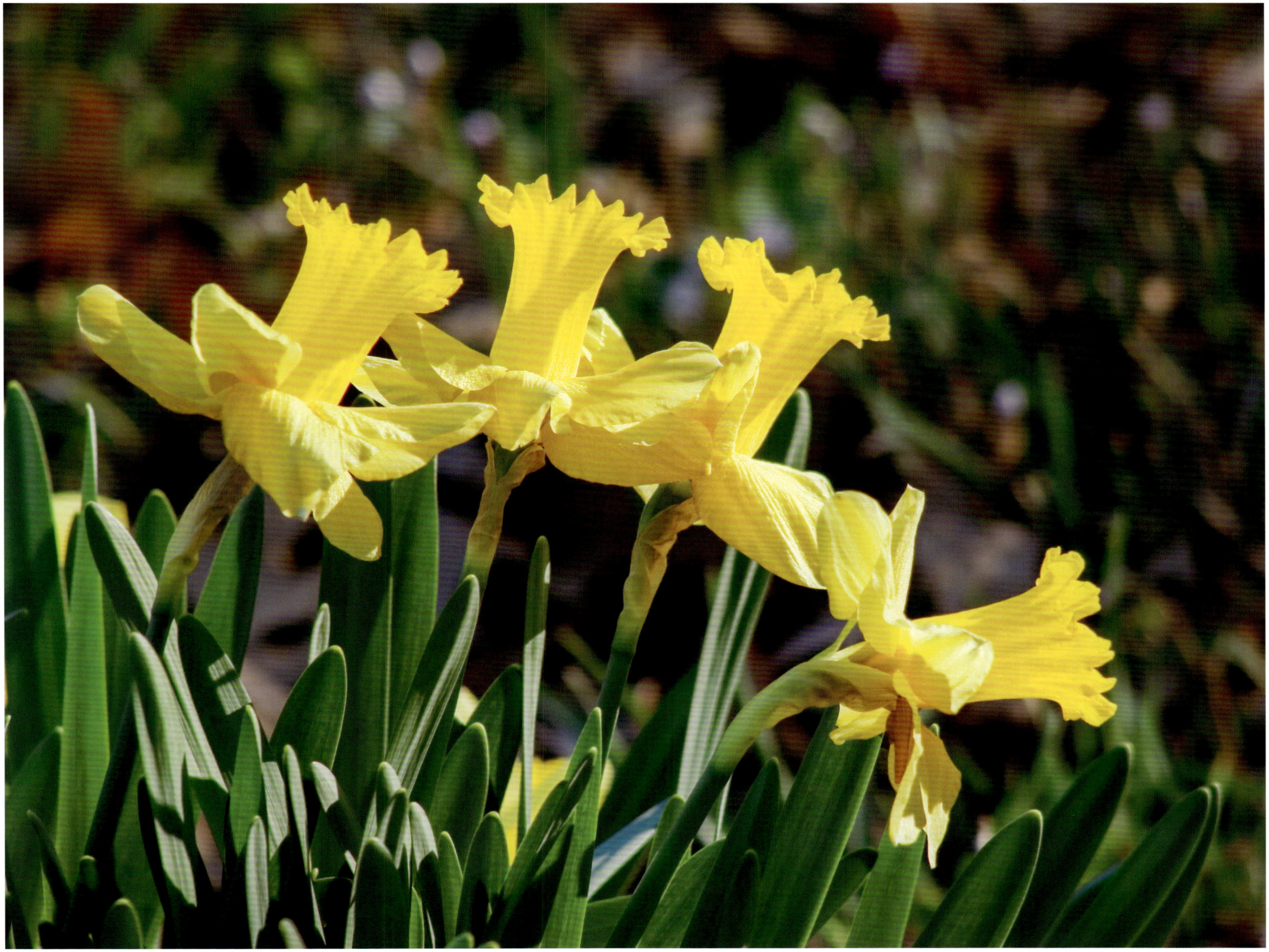

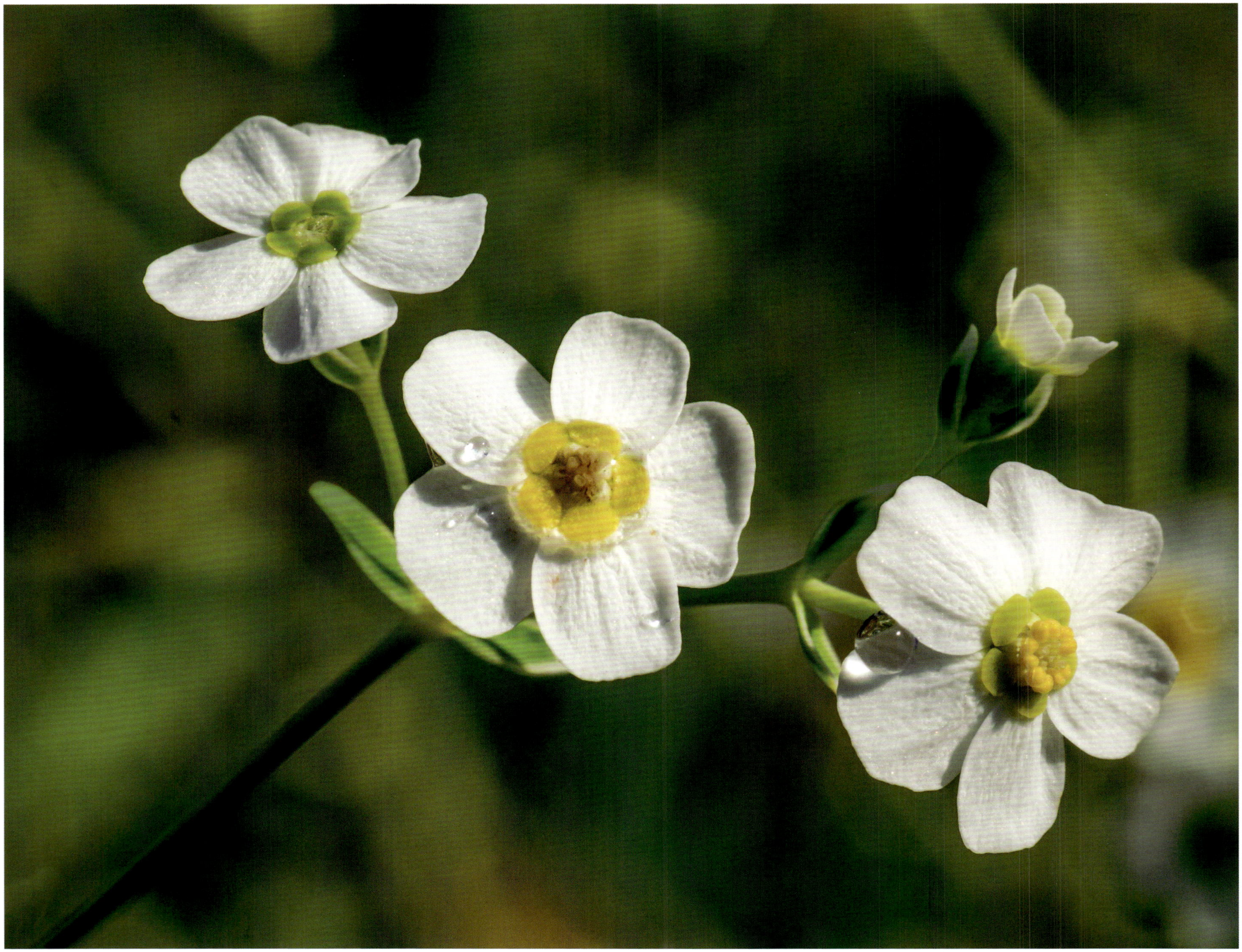

8. *Morning Dew on Flowering Spurge*, Meadow Lake, 2015
9. *Ash Tree*, North Side of Lake Marmo, 2017 (opposite)

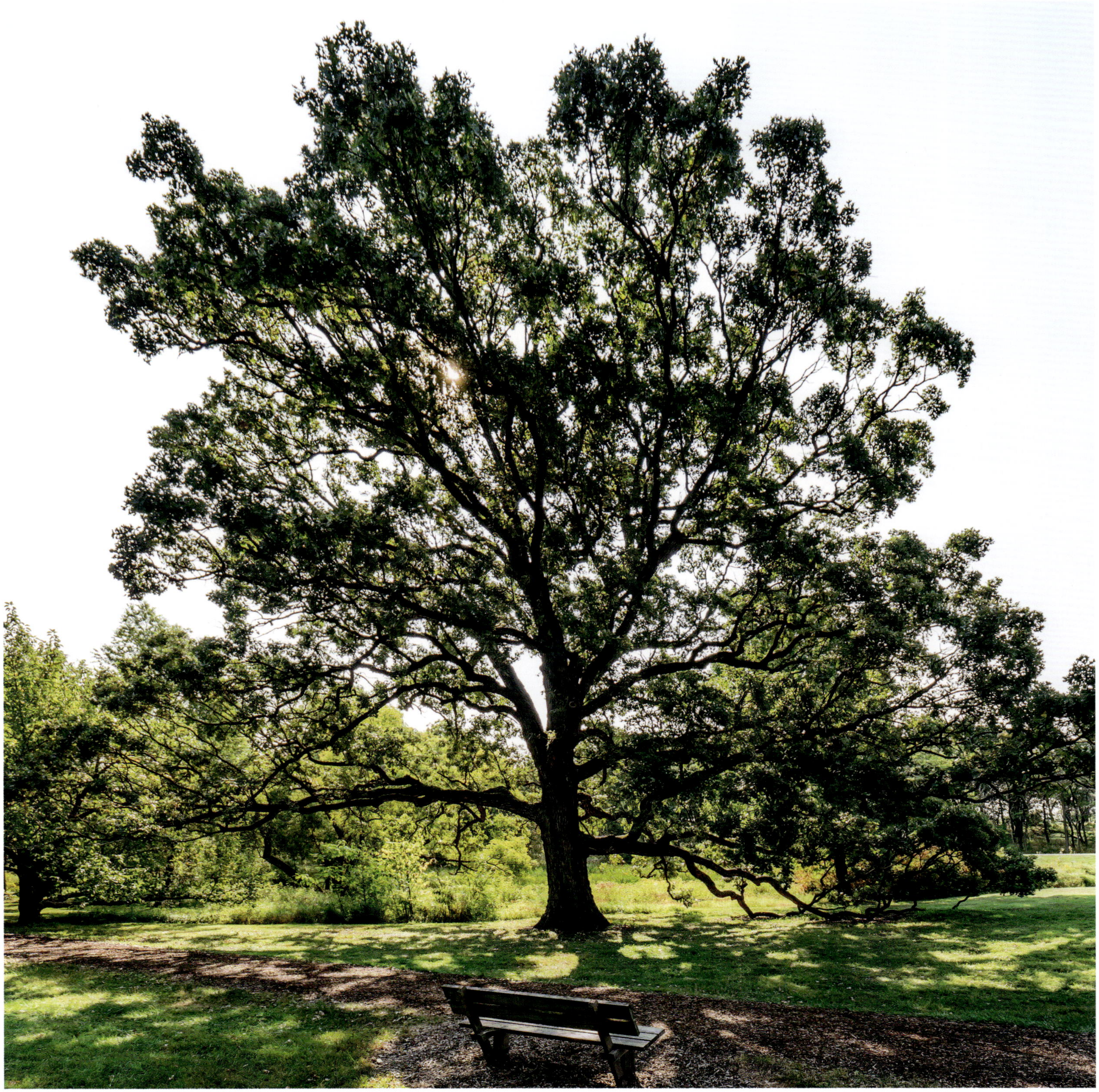

3

PLACE AND TIME

Finding the Right Time to Be at the Right Place

For many years three different stands of trees were my go-to places at The Morton Arboretum. And one of the three was my favorite—a small stand of pines on the north side of Meadow Lake. Each time I arrived at this location, I would slow my pace, take more time to walk around it, and occasionally stop to take a photograph or two.

Early on September 26, 1999, I walked to my favorite stand of pines and this time saw extraordinary light over the lake behind the trees. The light seemed to flood the scene and go on forever into the distance. My inner "feelings about what I'm seeing" started to surge. I looked through the camera to see what the camera was seeing. My feelings responded: "not quite right." So I moved a few feet back and looked again. Still not quite right. This time I took only one small half step to the left. Moving just inches away created a new place. The moment (the time) now felt right and the picture felt right. I clicked the shutter. *Cathedral Pines* (Plate 10) is my favorite of all my Arboretum pictures and a favorite of many. This place had been the right place for me for years. Now on this day, at this moment, the time was also right.

I can't go back and see what I loved about that time and place, but a worthy picture shows me what I felt at the time. And once I have one, there's the potential to return later for a new picture, for a double, and even for other multiples. Two weeks later, I returned to this same stand of pines and carefully stood at precisely the same location for a second picture (Plate 11). The place and the trees in both pictures are identical. But because the time had changed, this second picture has an entirely different mood, feeling, and meaning. Doubles and other multiples fascinate me, as this book testifies.

Painters start with a blank canvas and add lines, shapes, and colors to create their art. Photographers don't have that freedom. We start with a full canvas (screen) that is often a jumble. To find a picture—a picture that will live, a picture people will love—I need to take actions to, in effect, rearrange the lines, shapes, and colors so my picture distills what I am feeling here, in this place at this time.

Place and time are two simple but powerful controls I have to affect a photograph. In nature photography, I can't move the objects around in front of me. But I can change how they appear by moving my place (even by a few inches) or by waiting a few minutes (such as for a cloud to move), or returning another day, season, or even year. Plates 13 and 14 are examples, showing the same two oak trees in pictures taken four years apart and from opposite directions along the same small road.

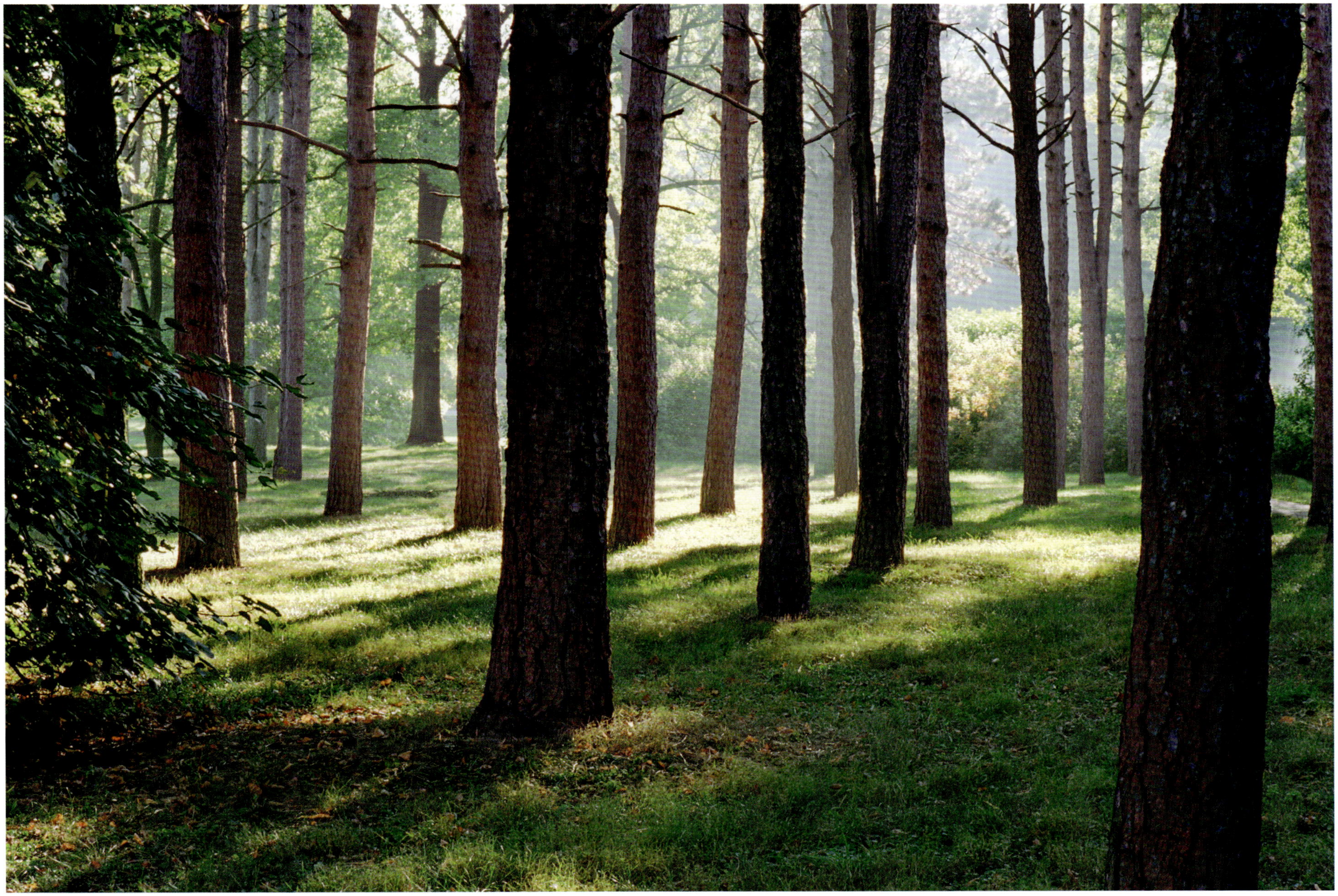

10. *Cathedral Pines, Old Meadow Lake, September 1999*

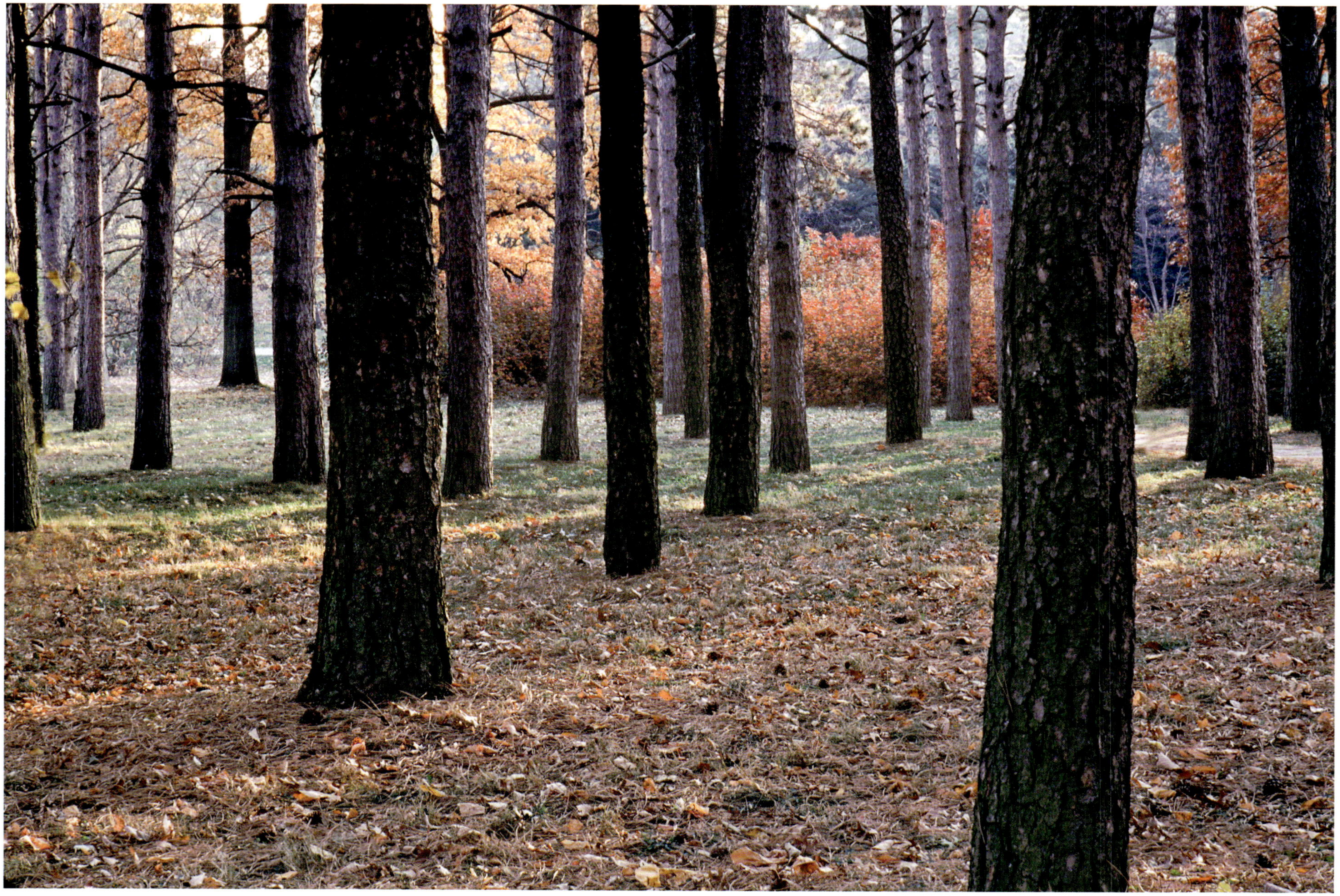

11. *Cathedral Pines, Old Meadow Lake, October 1999*

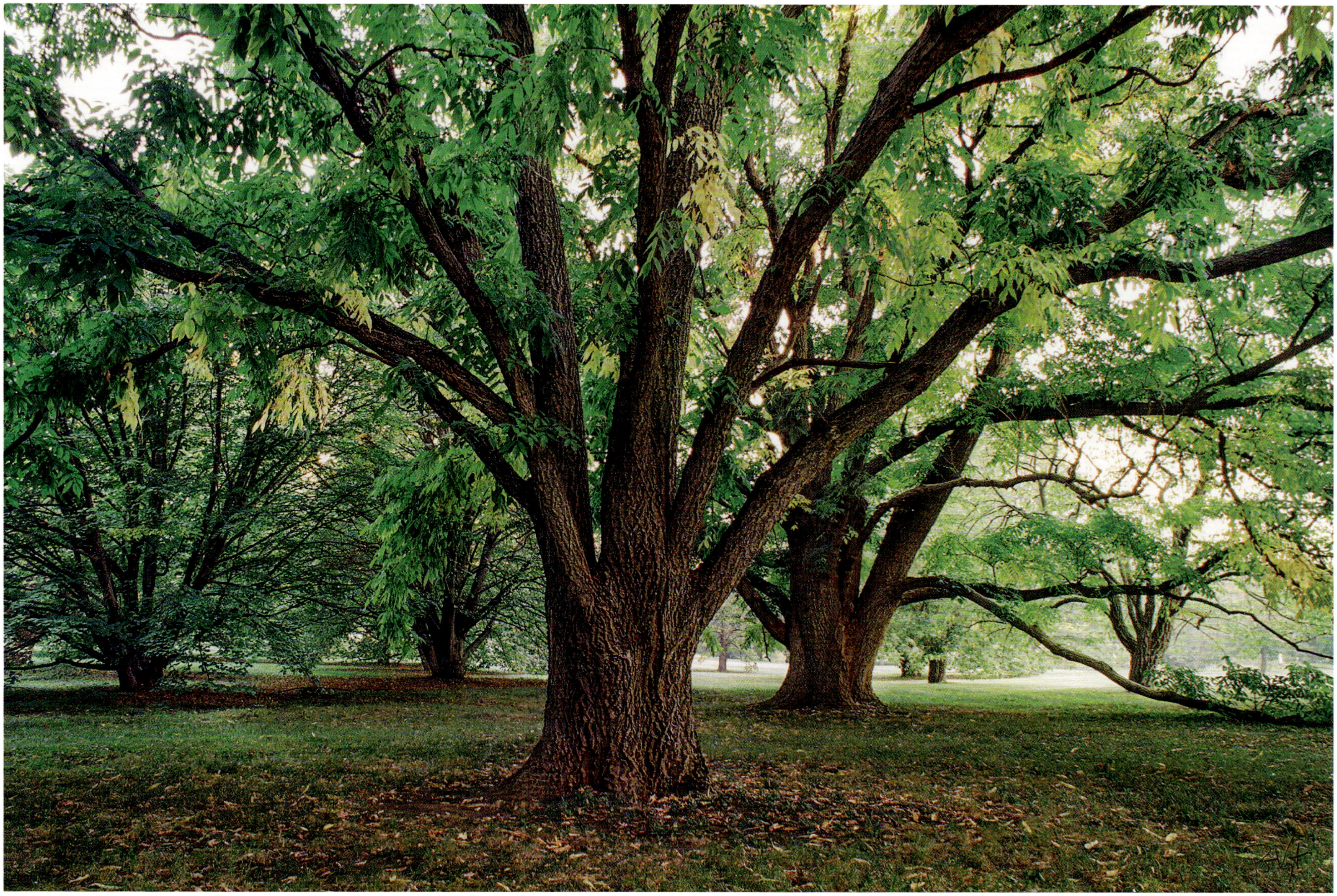

12. *Arching Cork Tree*, East Side, 1999

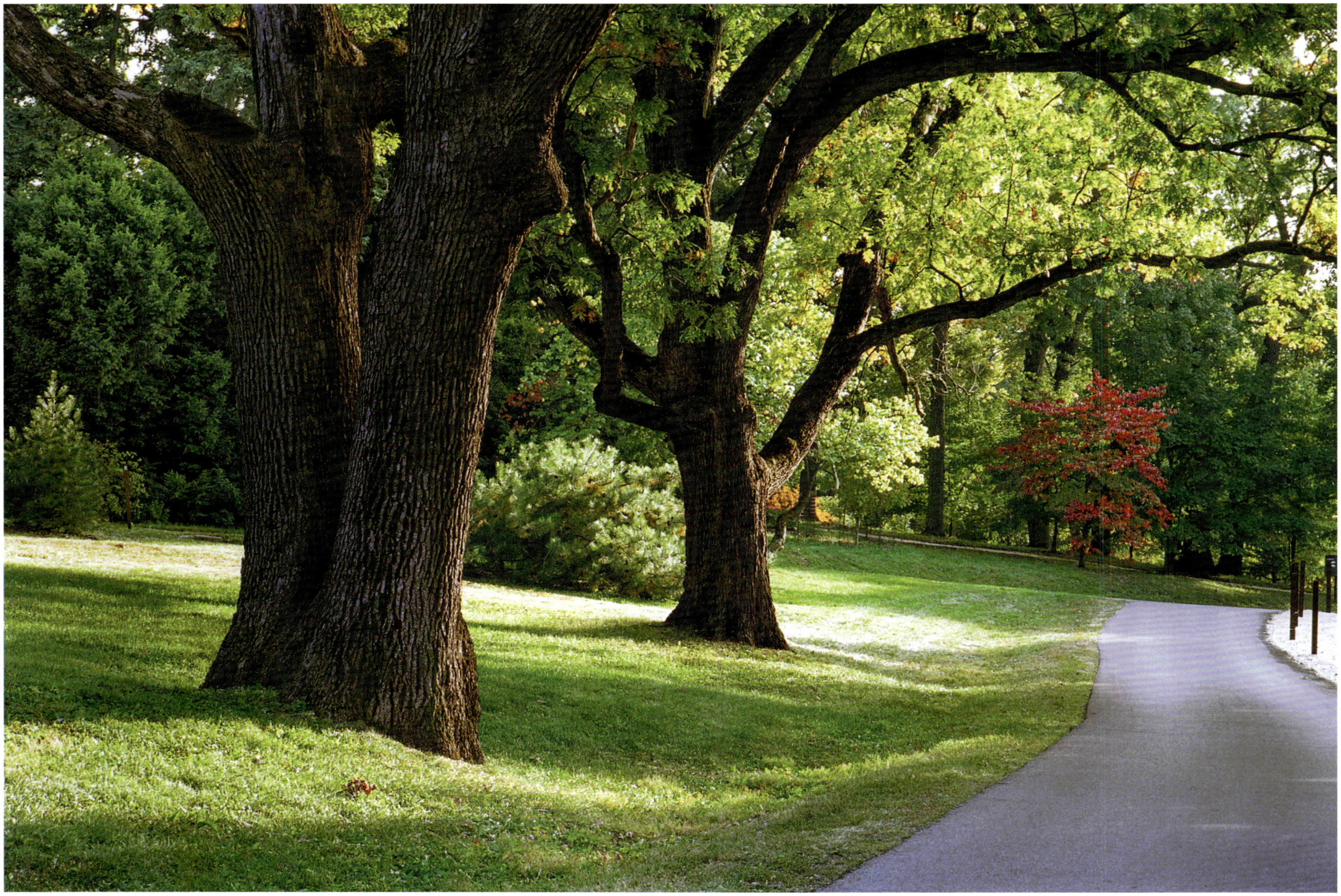

13. *Gallant Oaks*, East Side near Parking Area P17, 1999

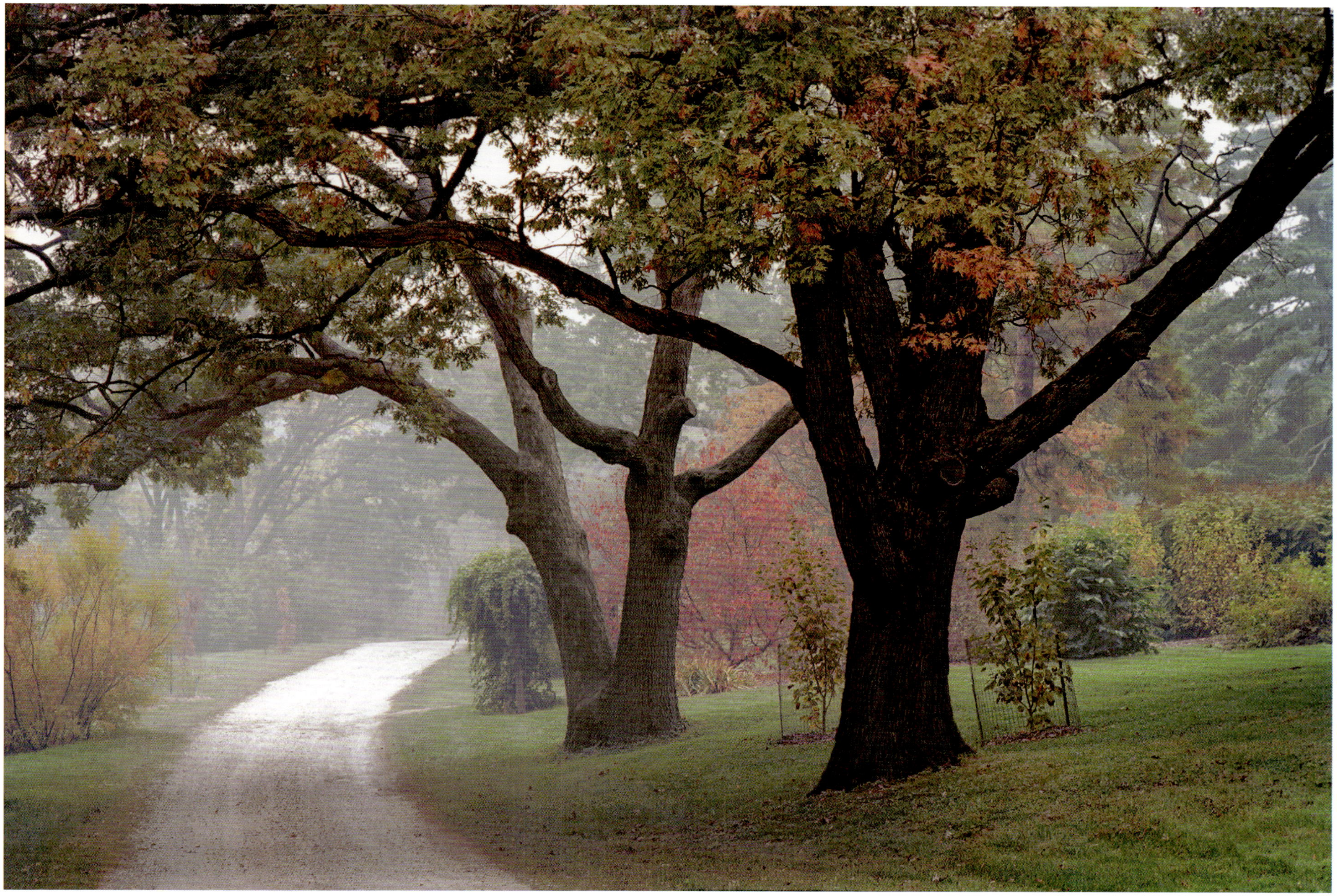

14. *Gallant Oaks in Light Rain*, 2003

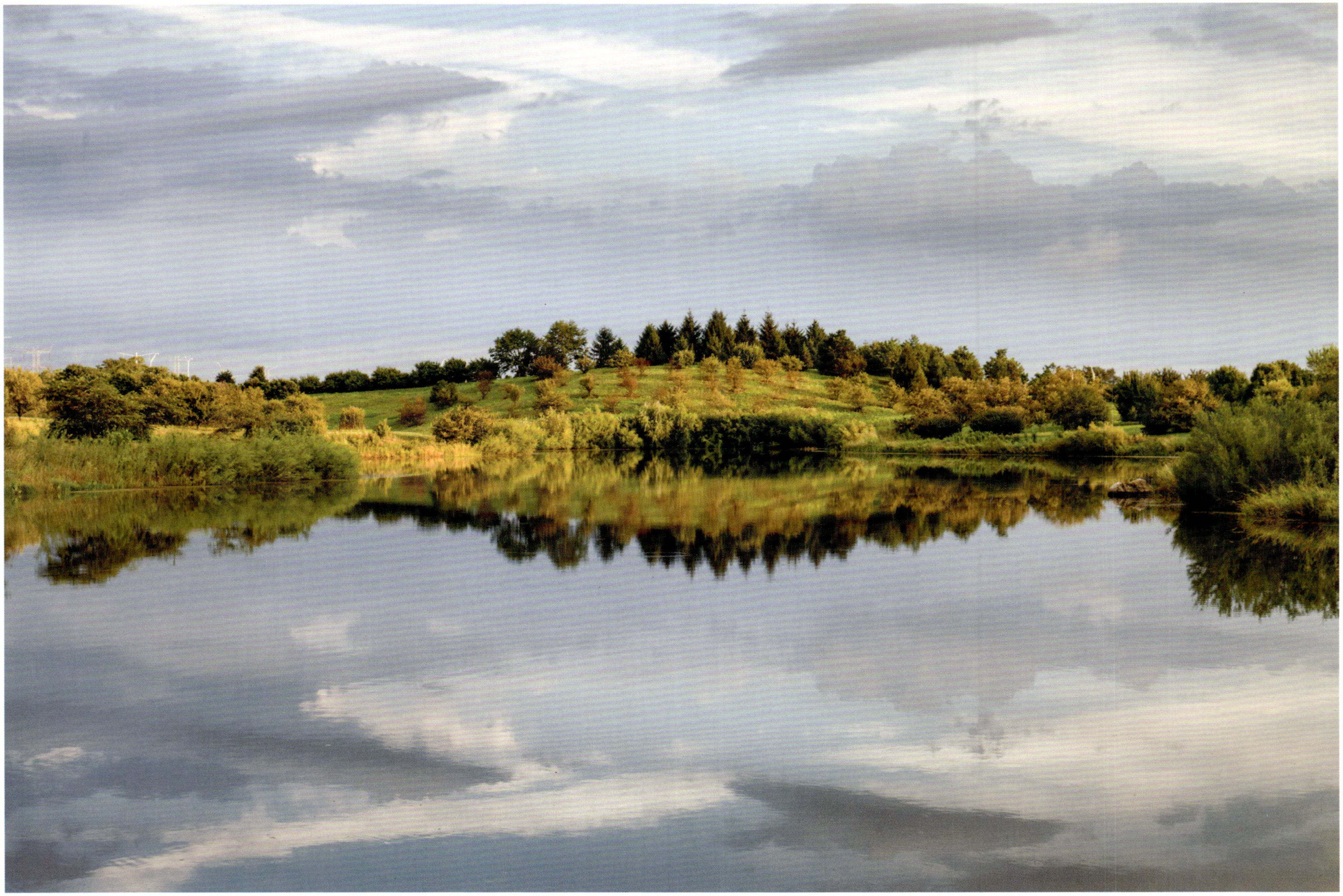

15. *Evening View South across Crabapple Lake*, 2011

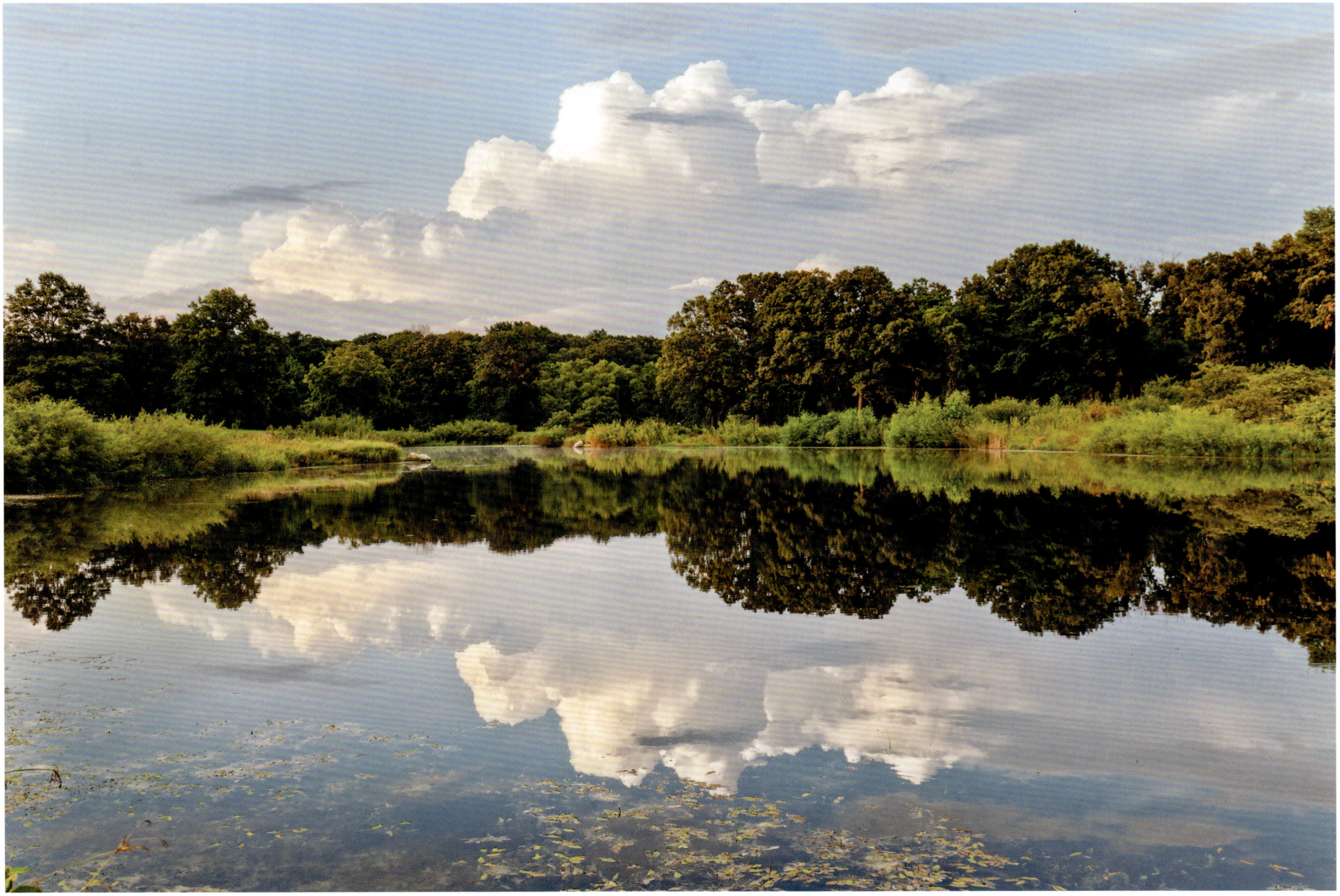

16. *Evening View North across Crabapple Lake*, 2011

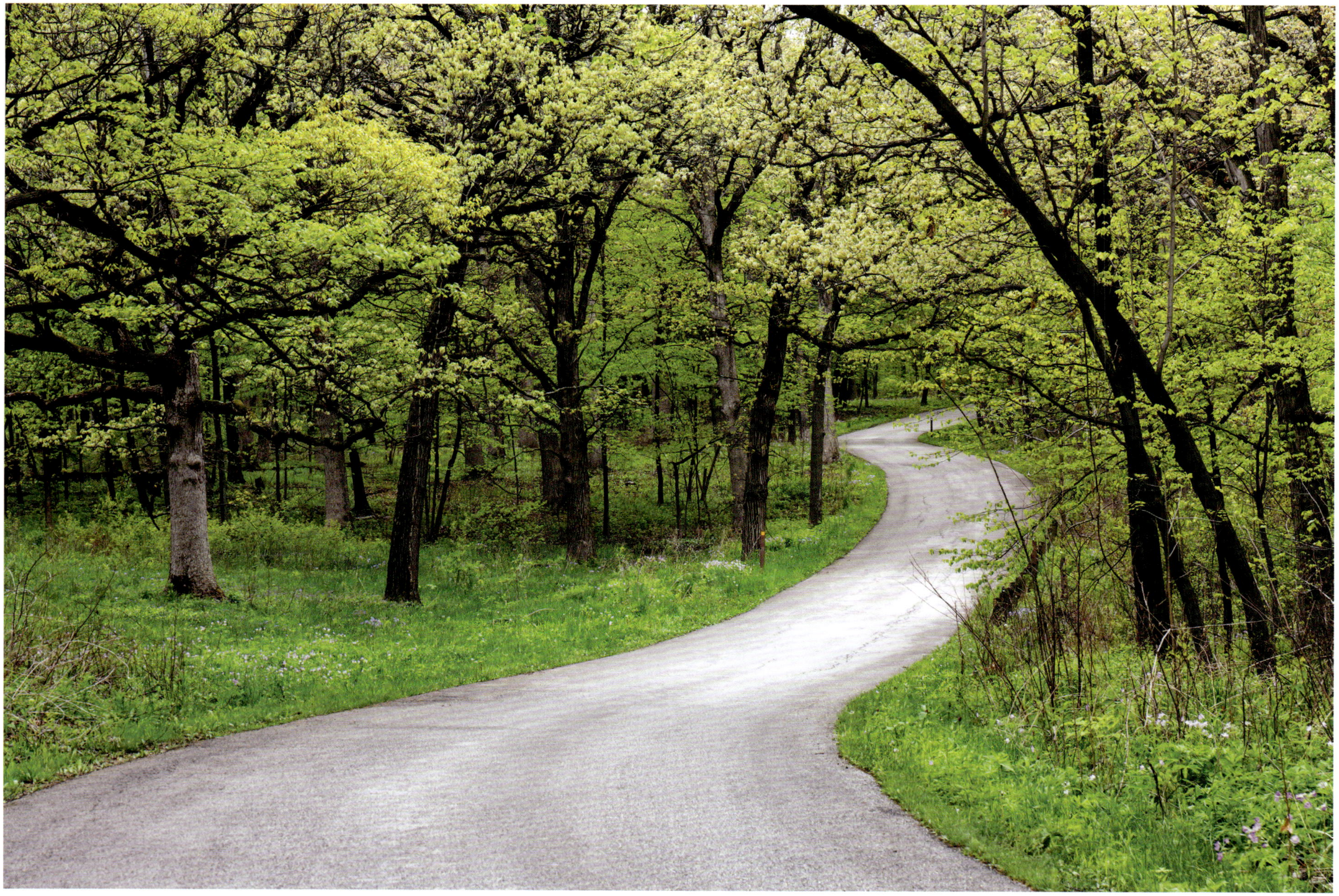

17. *Spring Green Comes to the Main Road*, East Side, 2017

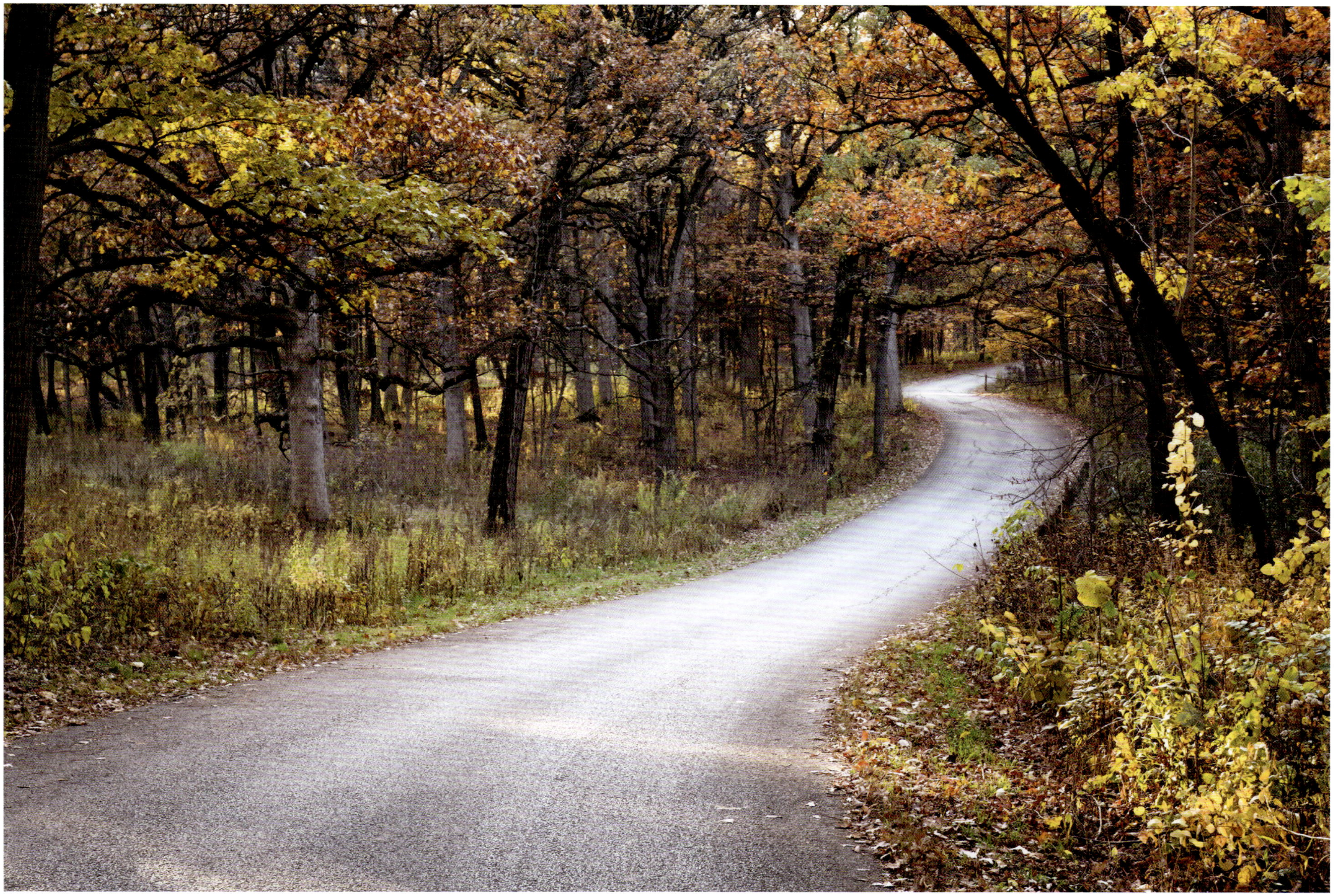

18. *Main Road*, East Side, November 2017

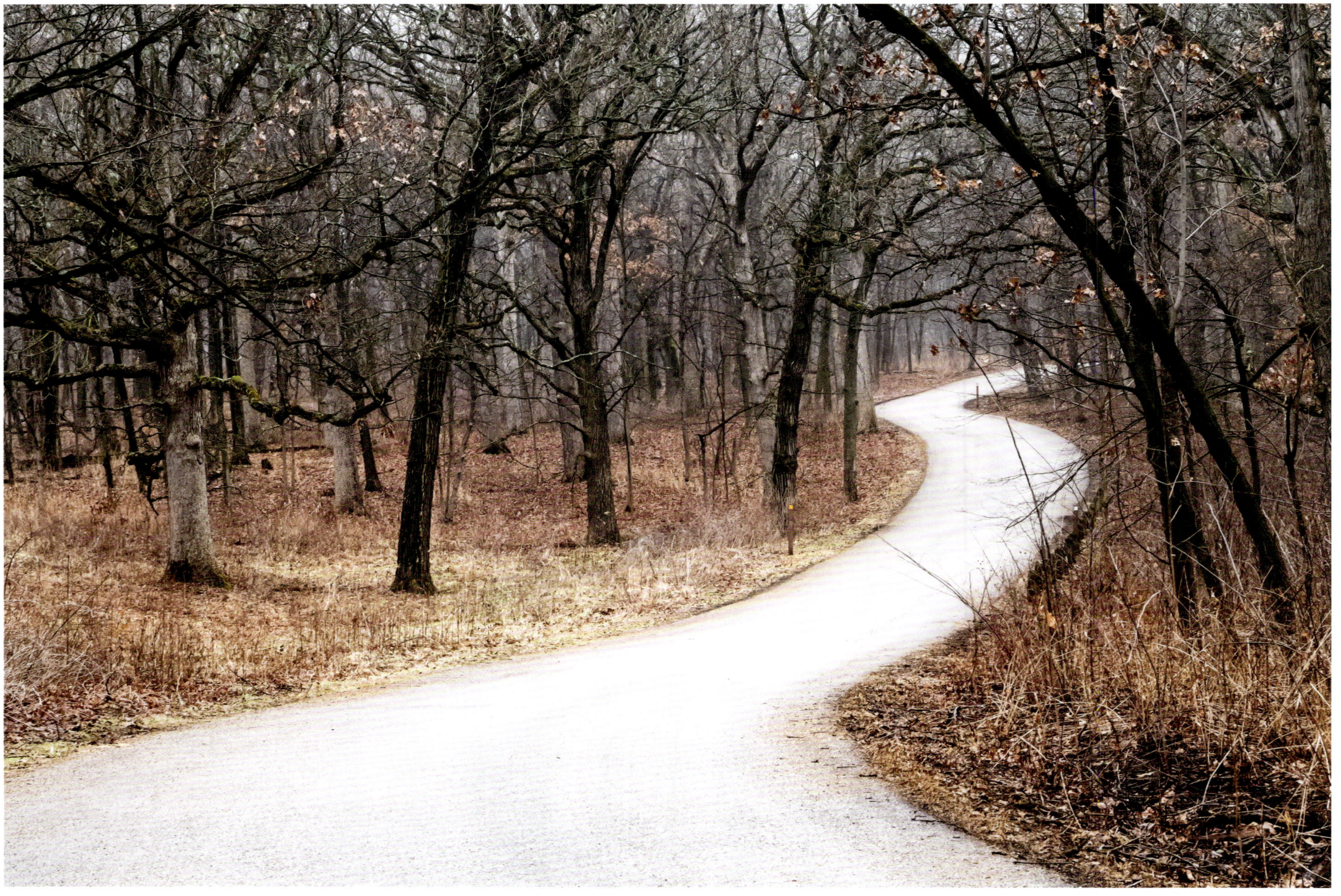

19. *Main Road, after the First Snow Melt*, East Side, January 2017

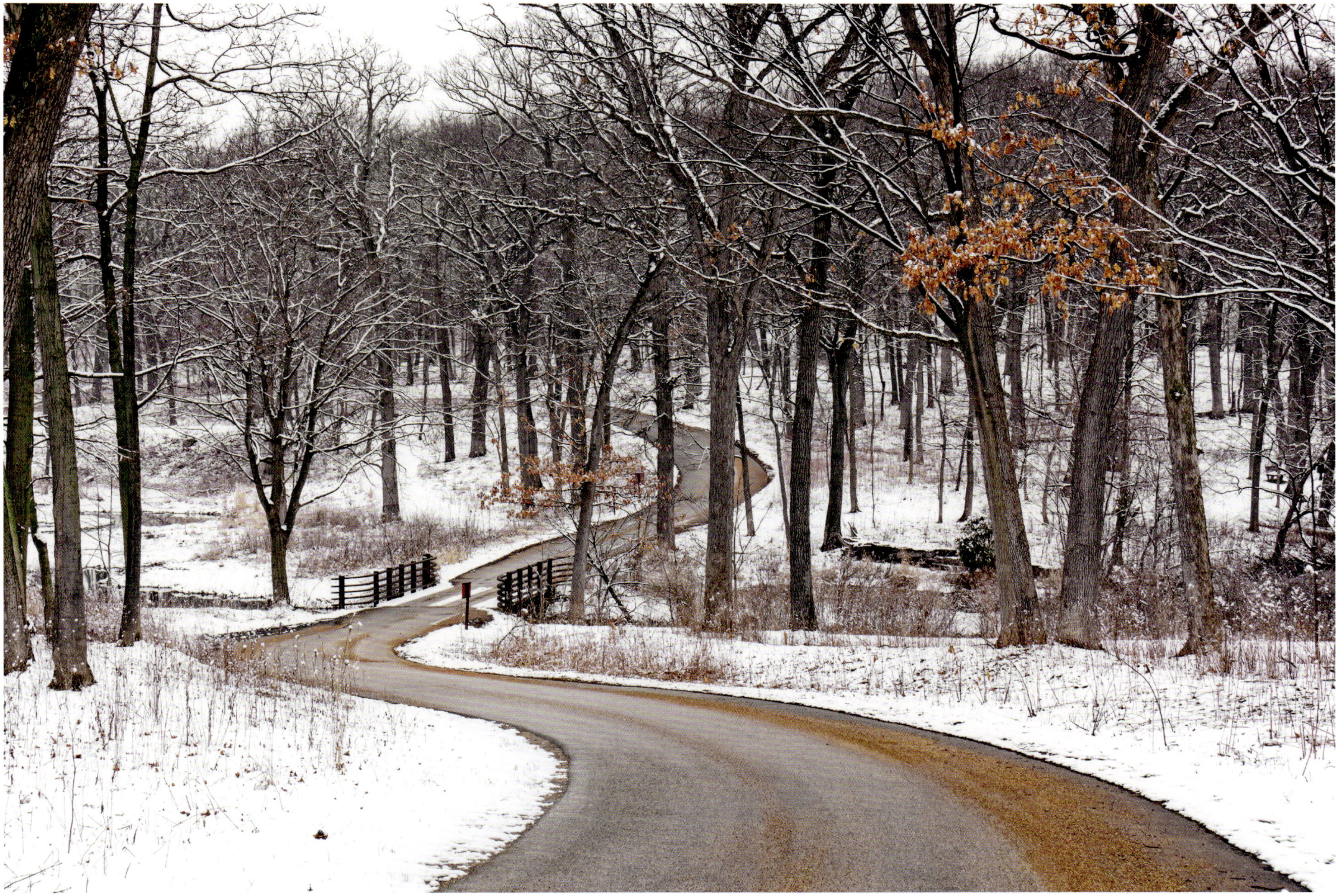

20. *Willoway Brook Bridge*, West Side, April 2018

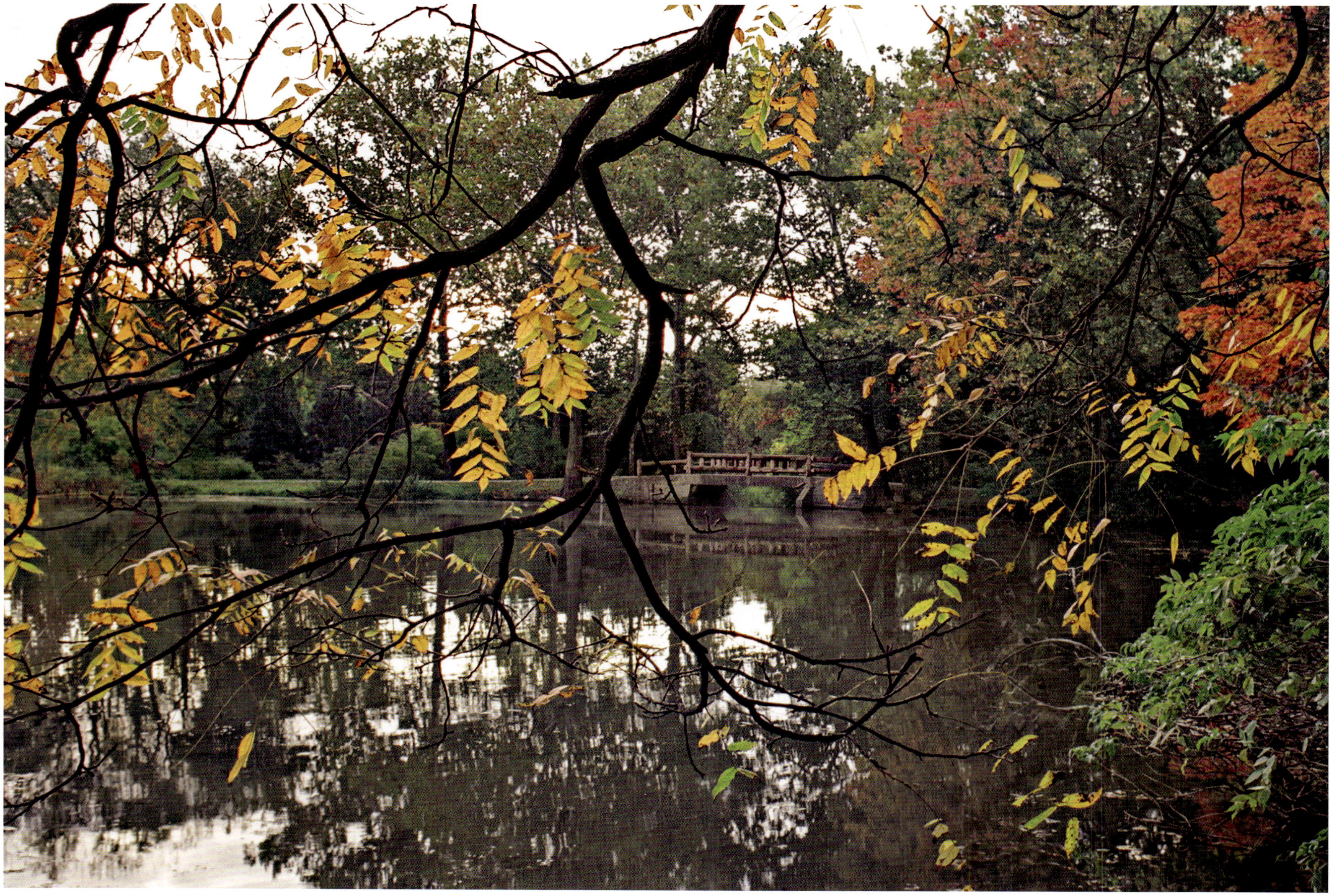

21. *Walnut Branches with Old Bridge*, Lake Marmo, 2000

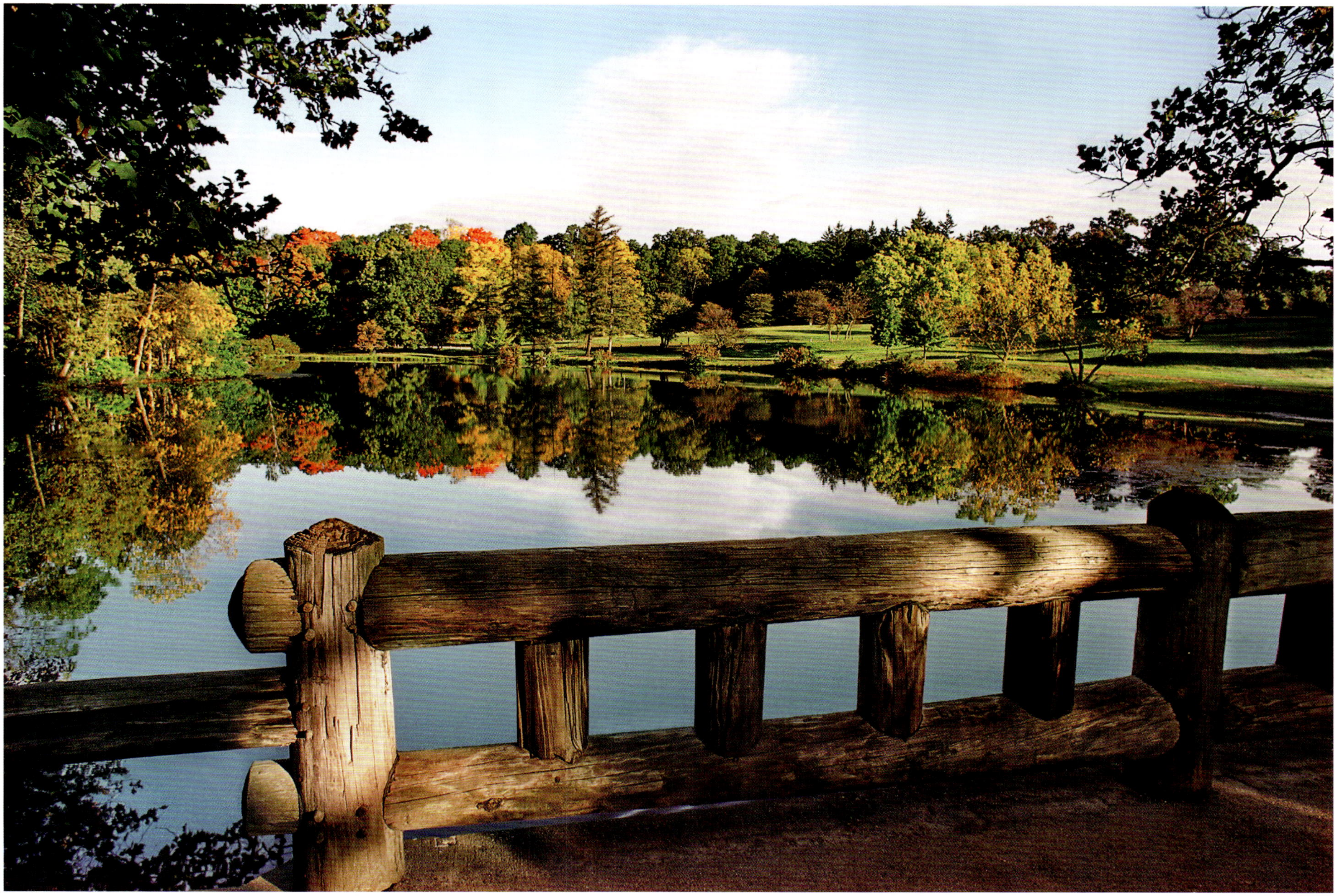

22. *Old Bridge at Rainbow Falls*, Lake Marmo, 1999

4

WAITING FOR THE PICTURE

By Returning Year after Year and Day after Day

It's impossible to overestimate how many people anticipate the sight of the beautiful redbud trees blooming in early May along the north shore of a little lake called Lake Marmo (Plate 23).

Every first week of May, I walk to this place as early in the day as I can, for as many days in a row as I can, to see this scene in as much of its fullness and beauty as I can. Not only the intensely pink redbuds, but also in some years, white dogwood flowers bloom right behind them. And on still mornings, we get to see these flowering trees doubled in reflections on the lake.

It's exquisite and joyful to be there and see this sight. But there's a challenge to finding a picture that can even match such a beautiful scene. My search, year after year, was to find a picture that could transcend the scene's prettiness, a picture with a circular song inside it offering something personal to me and to others every time we look at it.

On May 1, 2004 (the fifth year I'd been returning to this location), just after 7 A.M., as I walked down the path toward the lake, I could see light breezes slightly rippling the surface of the water and delightful abstractions of the trees, blossoms, and colors reflecting on the lake.

That morning when I reached a point directly opposite the redbud trees, a mallard duck landed in the water off to my left and began to leisurely paddle across the lake. I quickly set up my camera and watched the mallard's progress and the growing quicksilver wake trailing behind him.

As the mallard paddled, the wake line grew. When the duck reached a point in front of me, I clicked the shutter, though I knew that moment was not yet the right moment.

"Keep going," I breathed to myself, clicking the shutter again.

"Please go straight; please don't slow down," I added, clicking once again.

A few moments later, I knew—I could feel it—the mallard had reached the right place and I clicked the shutter one final time. The picture I found that day is *Mallard Crossing Lake Marmo on May Day* (Plate 23).

I love this picture because it reveals the magical, thrilling moment I experienced inside a very full scene. The mallard and silver wake brought something more to the beautiful trees and their reflections. I treasure this picture as a gift to me for my commitment to the place, for returning year after year, and for patiently waiting until the right time for this picture.

Every year since, in early May, I have walked down to the lake to see and feel the explosion of spring once again and to take a few photographs. The mallards and female ducks I now see on the lake are progeny of the mallard I saw in 2004. While it's the same location, the trees have grown, and some have fallen. Both the place and the time are different. I keep looking to try to feel my way to another picture here. So far, none has matched the magic I felt and found on May Day 2004, as one particular mallard crossed Lake Marmo.

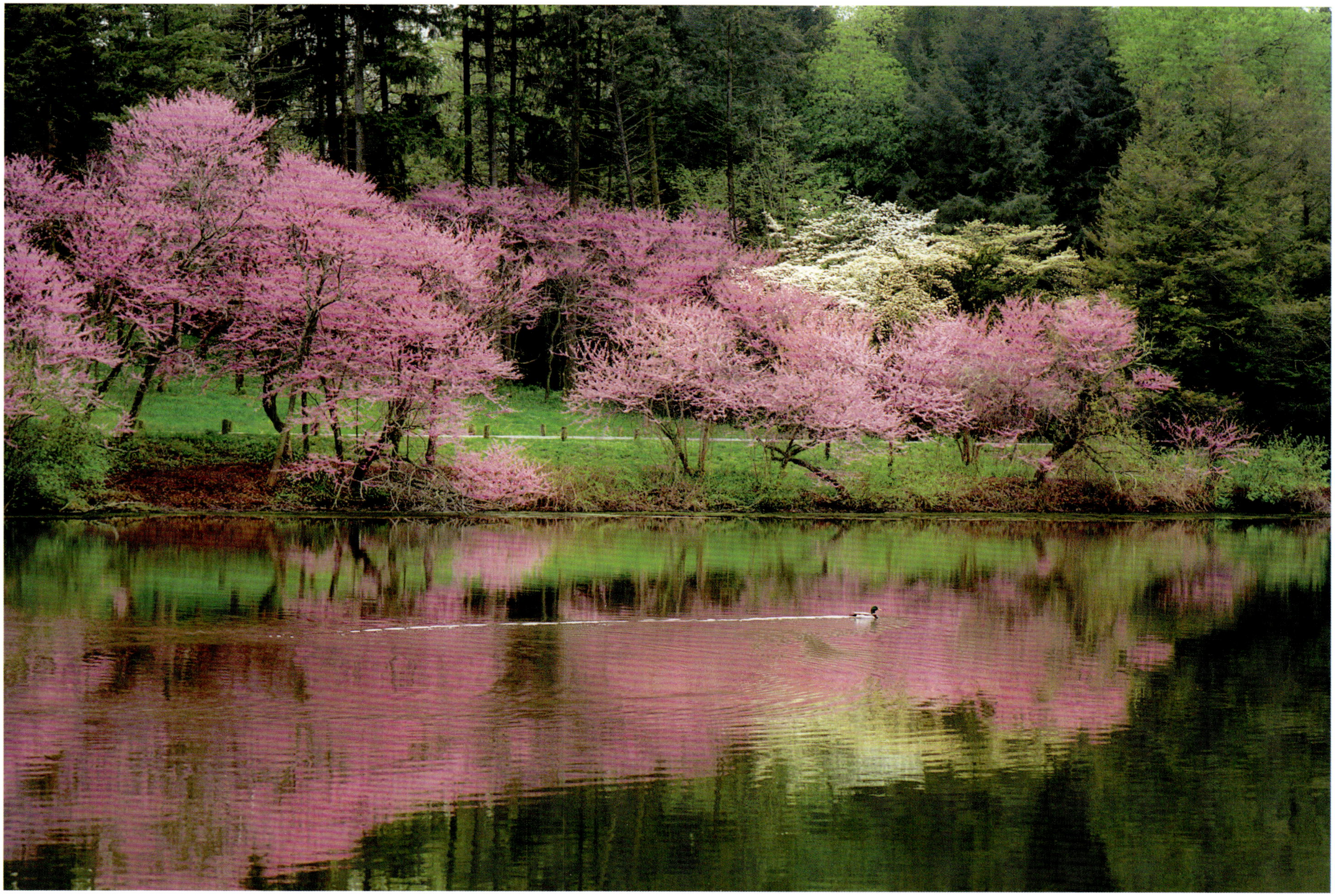

23. *Mallard Crossing Lake Marmo on May Day*, 2004

5

WAITING FOR THE PICTURE

By Staying Longer

The *Canada Geese on Meadow Lake* (Plate 24) first caught my attention. But *Meadow Lake Rendezvous* (Plate 25) is the picture I waited for. Both were taken one morning at Meadow Lake near the Visitors' Center. It was September 15, 2007. I arrived, as I often do, as soon as the Arboretum gate opened. It had been quite warm for several weeks, so the lake water was warm. The chilly night air over the warm water now caused a mist to rise from the lake. Indeed, even before entering the park, I had seen spires of mist extending above the trees between me and the lake. As I reached the lake and started walking along the path, I kept watching this ethereal mist swirling and drifting across the lake and extending fifteen to twenty feet up above the water. Soon, two Canada geese gliding around the lake caught my attention. I found a spot at the west end of the lake and stopped to watch them.

Over the next forty-five minutes, I took several dozen photographs while these two geese (and several ducks) circled and crisscrossed the water, adding their swirls to the base of the rising mist. Joggers passed me several times on their laps. I stayed still, entranced, and continued watching. At one point the two geese separated. Then they turned and swam back towards each other. As they got close one raised its head. It was the right moment and I was ready. *Meadow Lake Rendezvous* (Plate 25) is that picture.

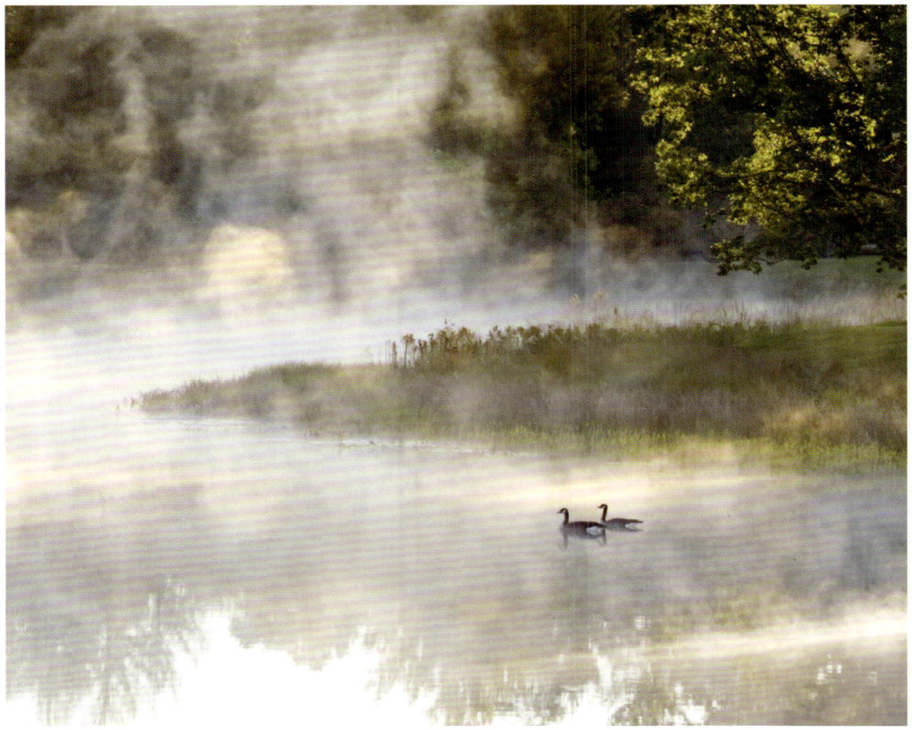

24. Canada Geese on Meadow Lake, September 2007

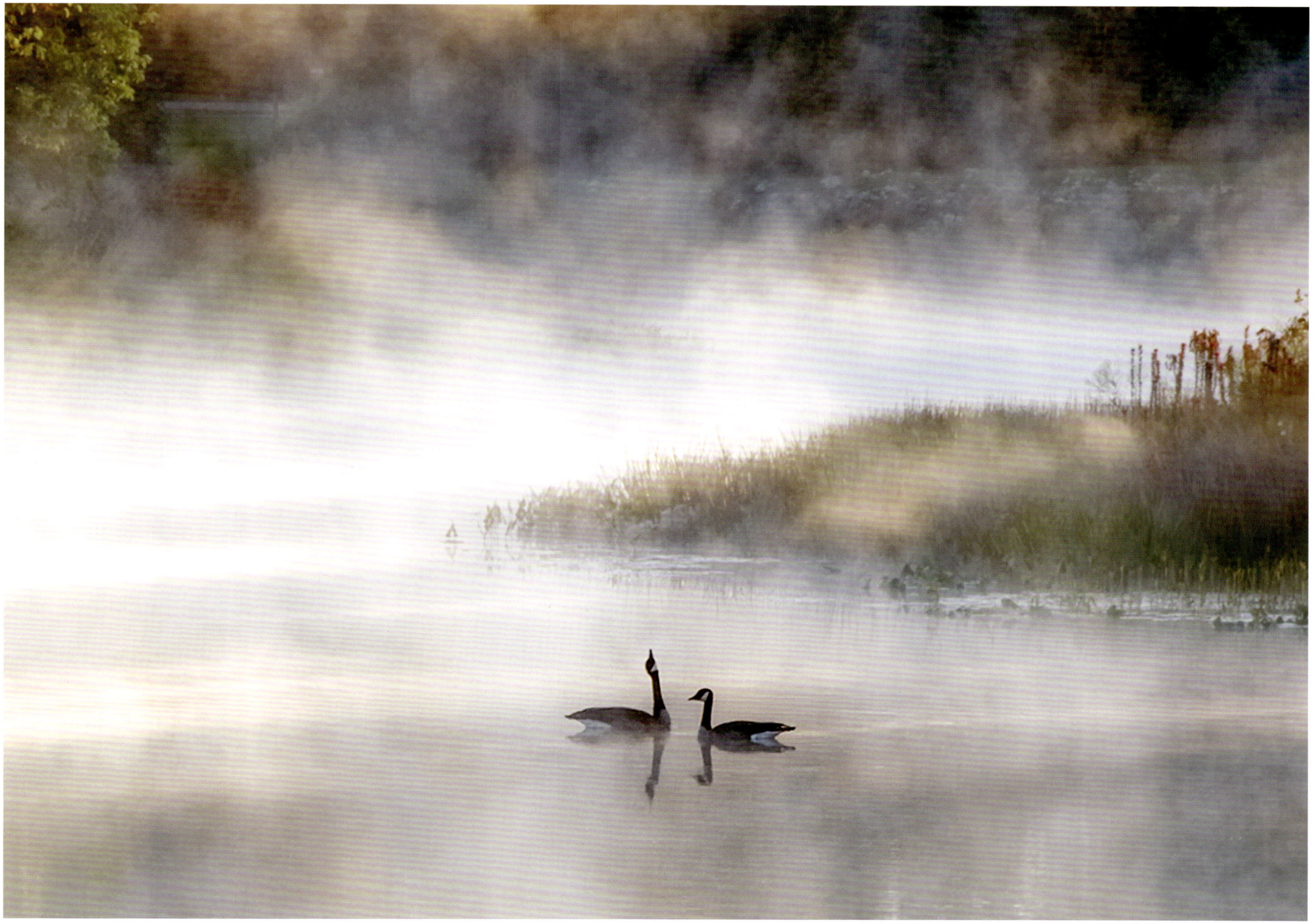

25. *Meadow Lake Rendezvous*, 2007

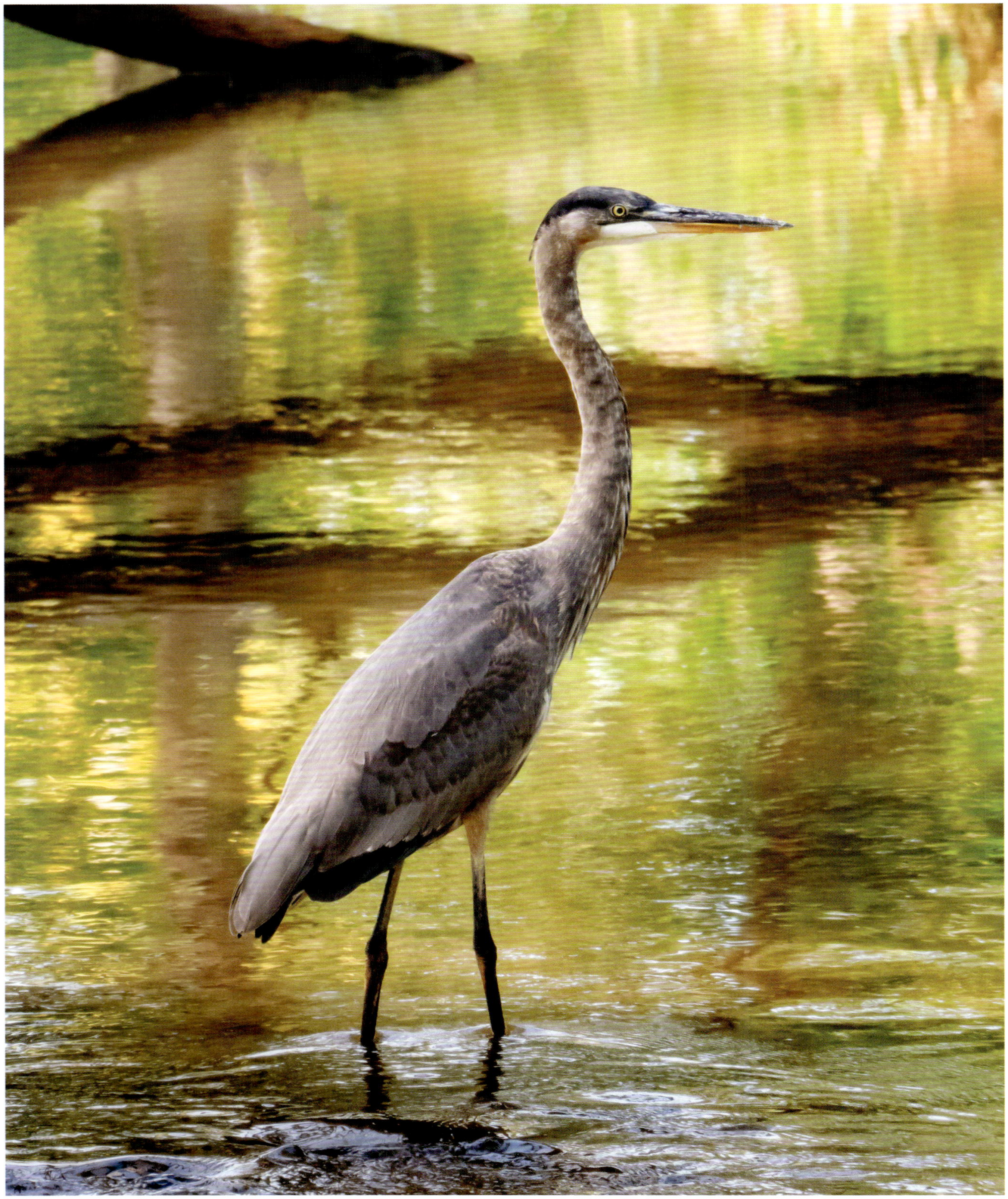

26. *Heron on Willoway Brook*, West Side, 2018
27. *Misty Morning on Lake Marmo*, 2017 (opposite)

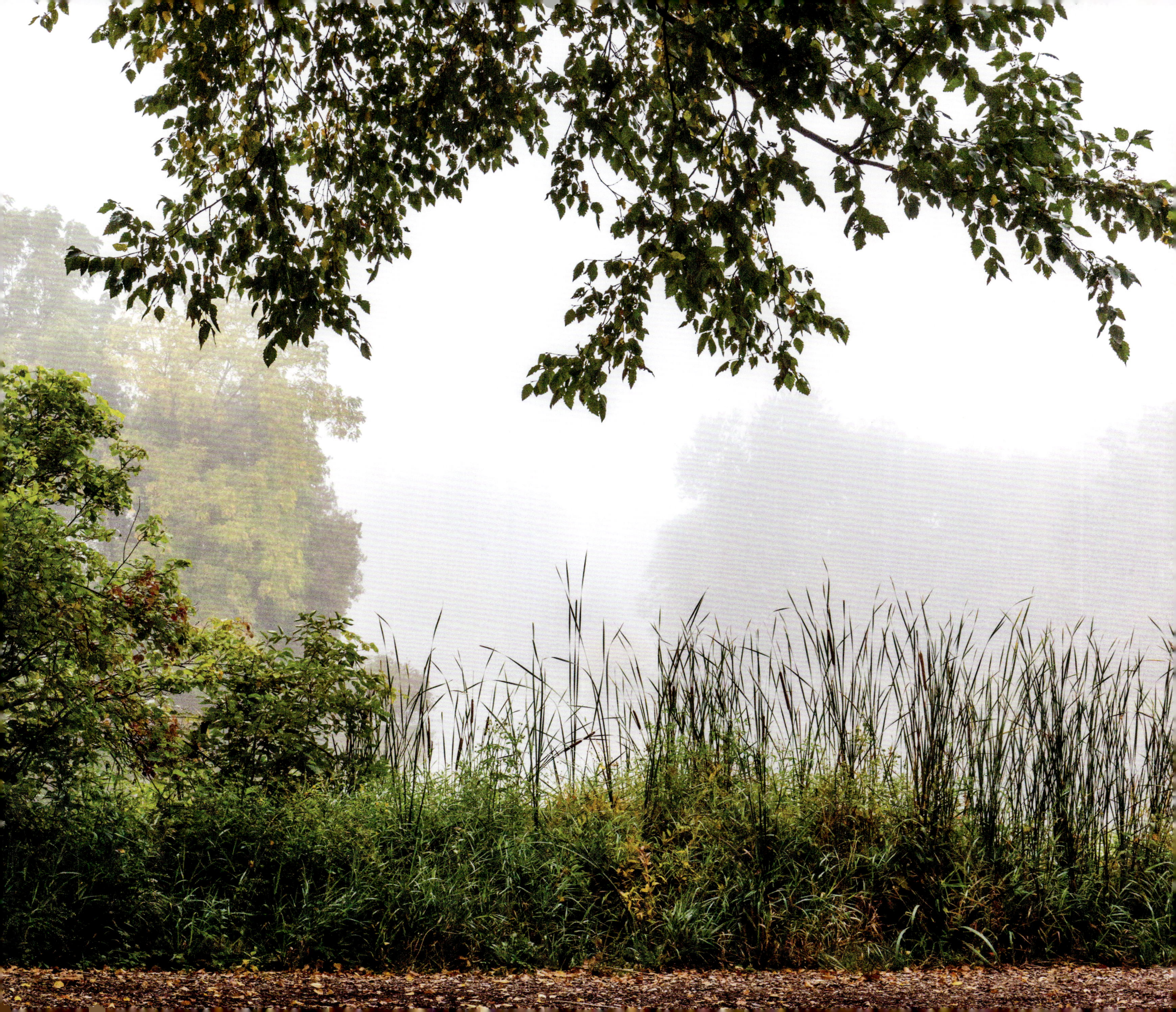

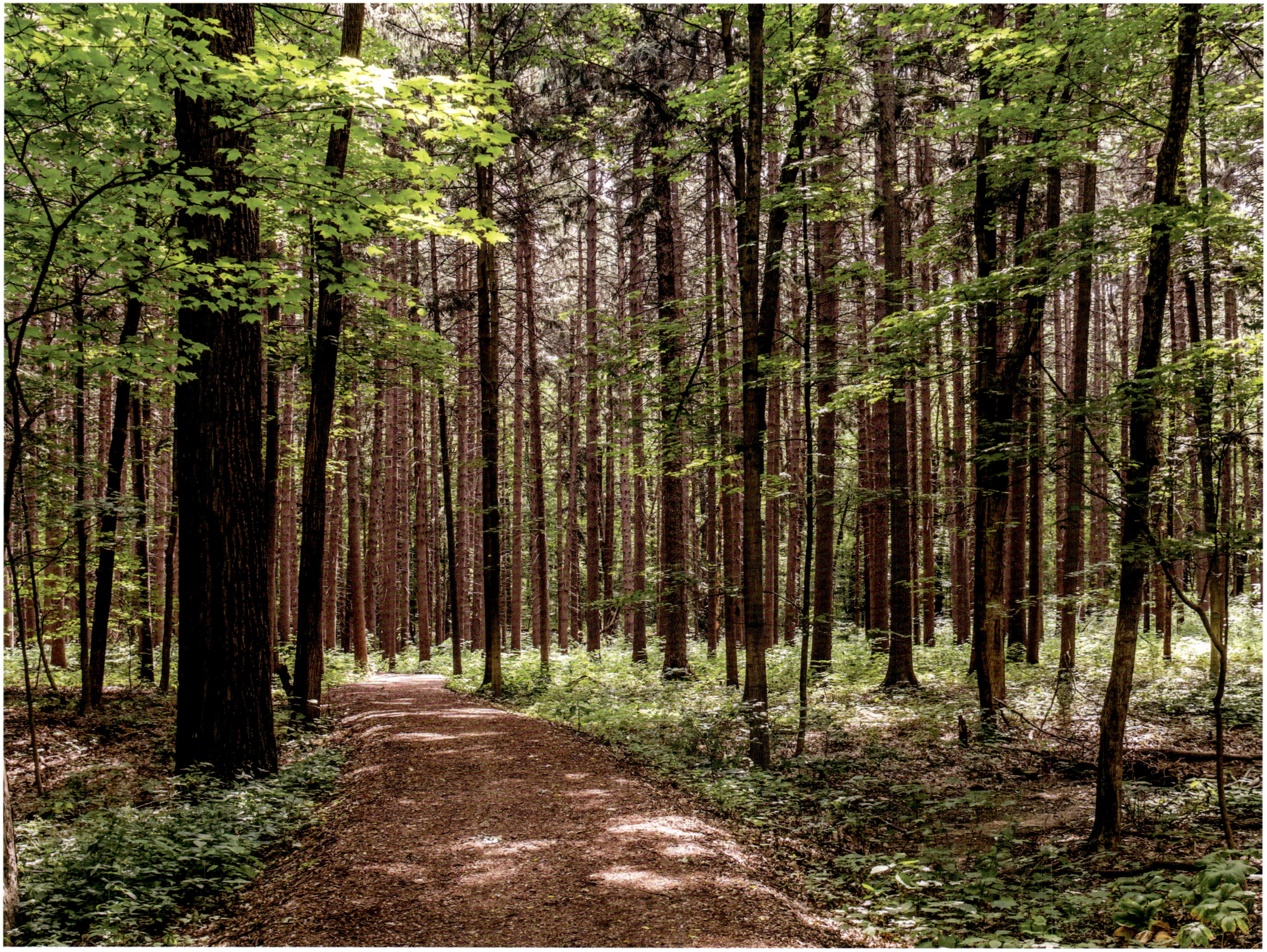

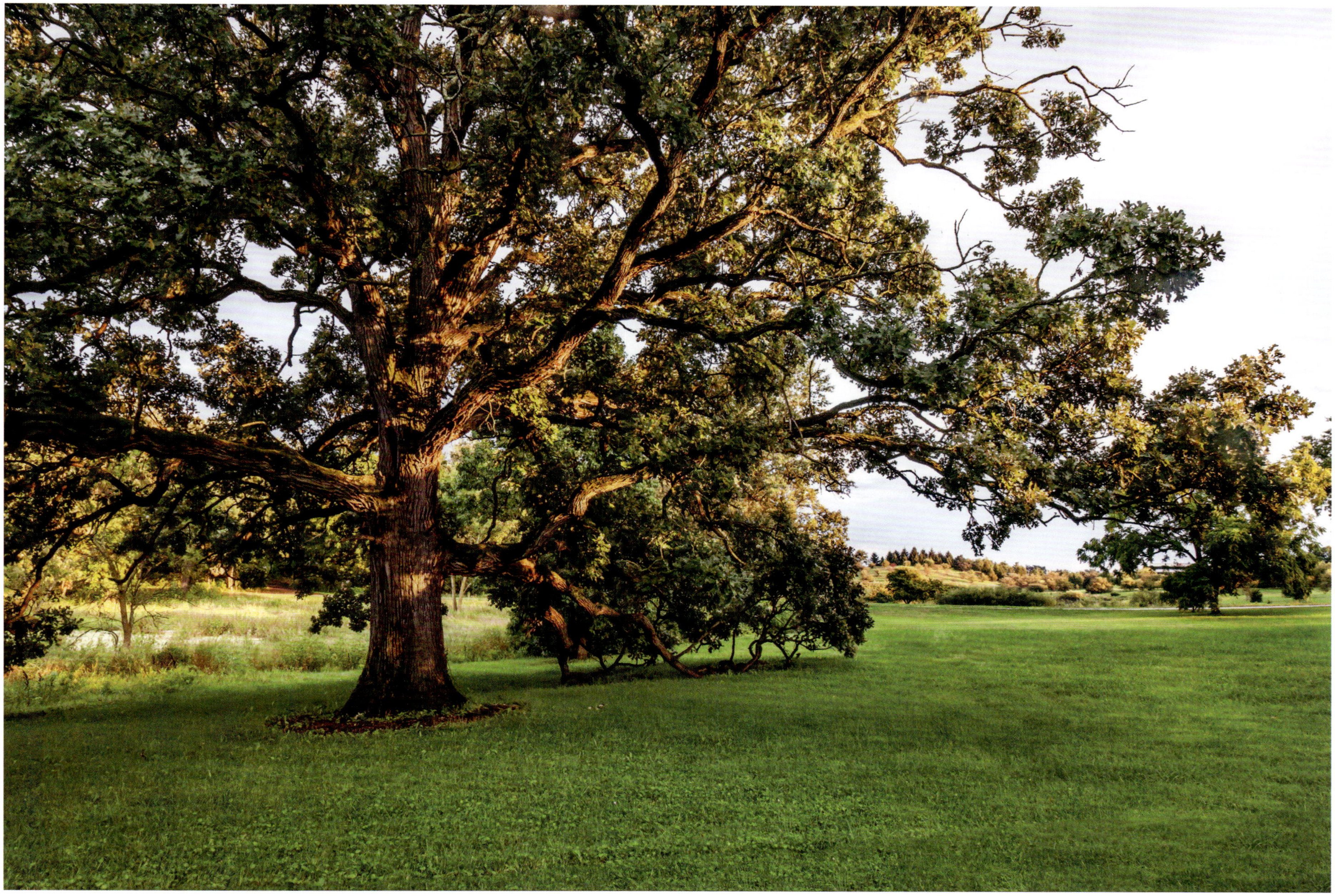

28. *Summer Sun Dappled Spruce*, 2017 (opposite)
29. *Great Oak at Sunset*, near Crowley Marsh, 2011

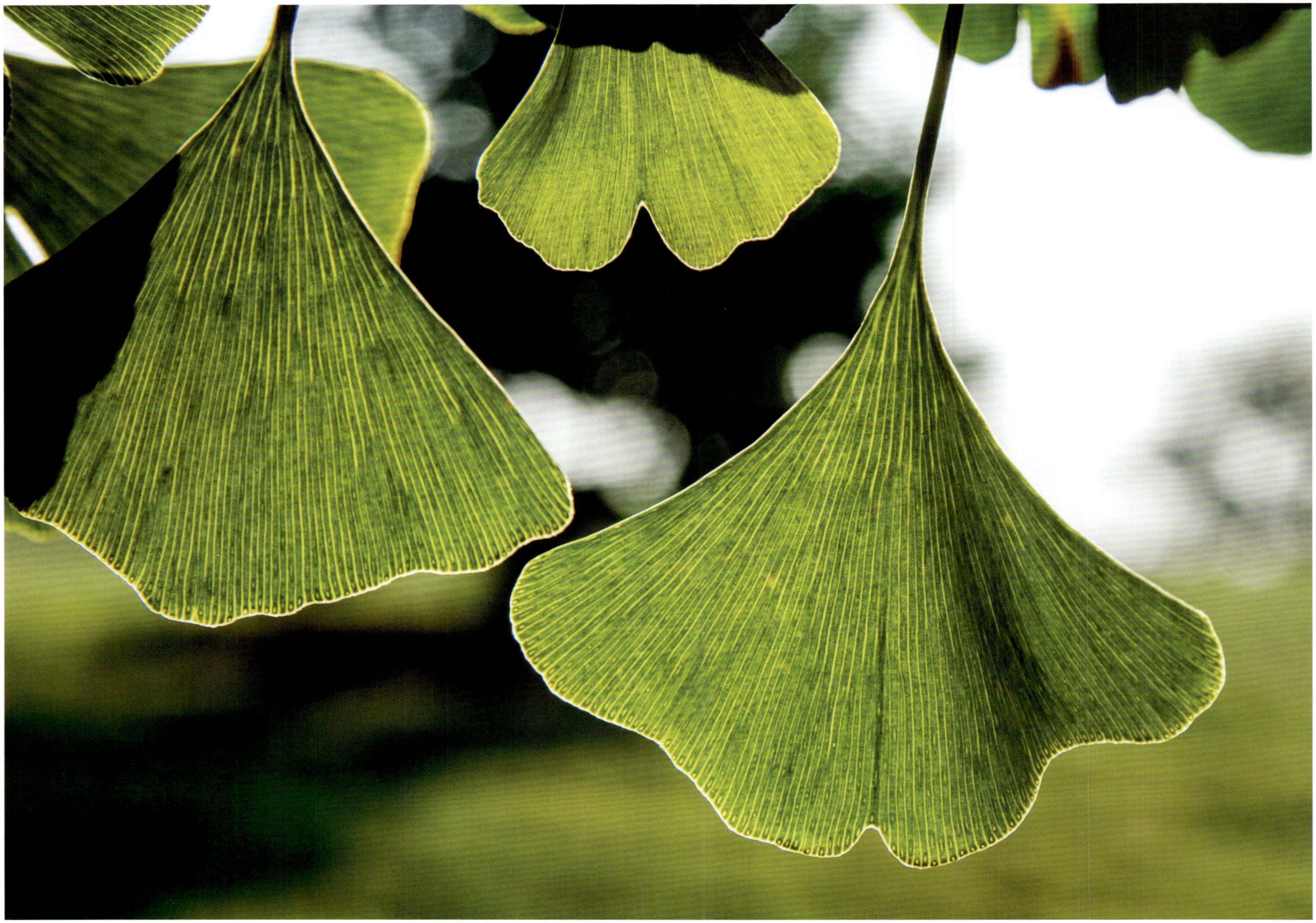

30. *Ginkgo Leaves along the Joy Path*, 2011

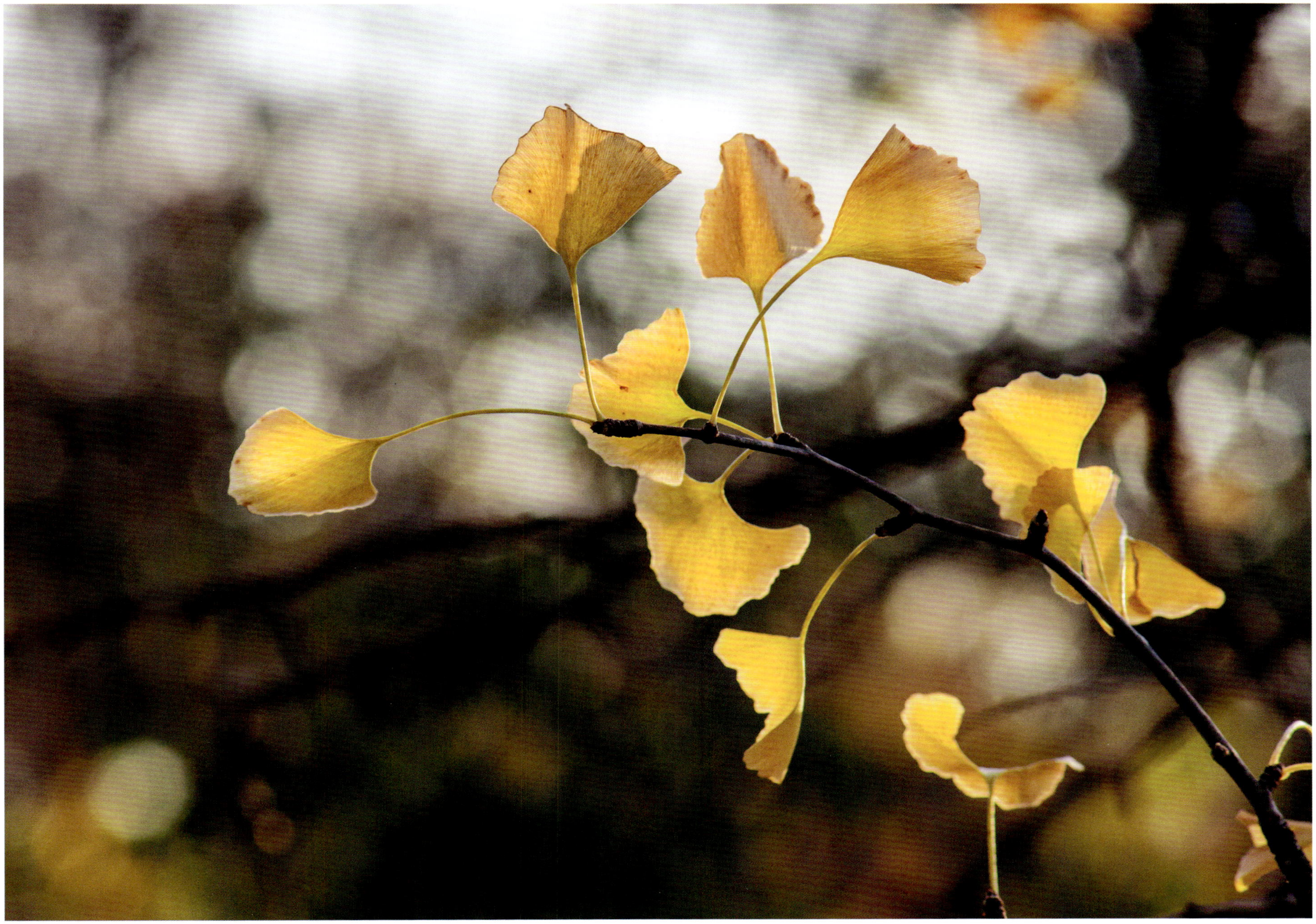

31. *Ginkgo Branch*, Japanese Garden, 2014

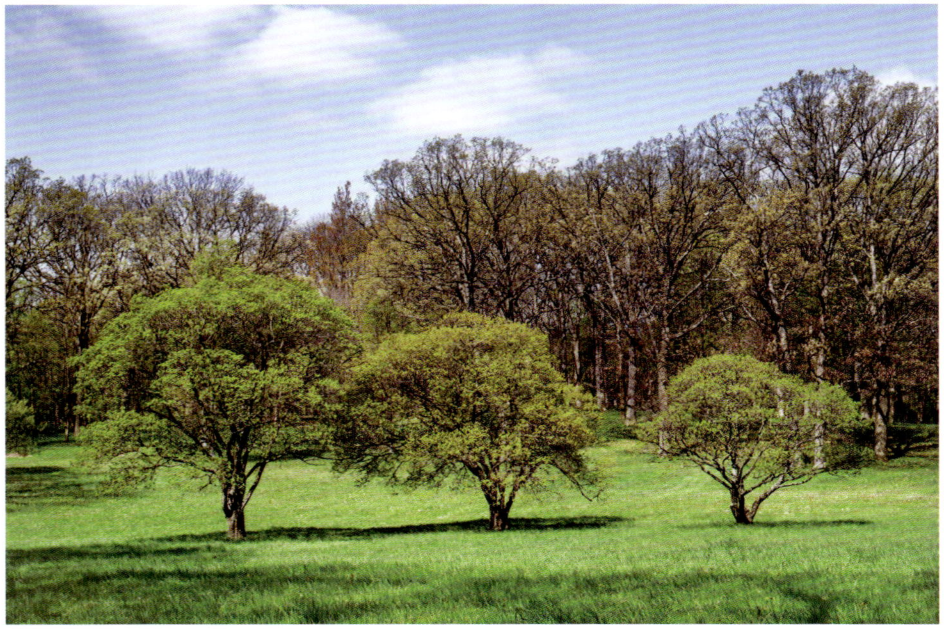

32. *Three Maple Trees, Spring 2005*

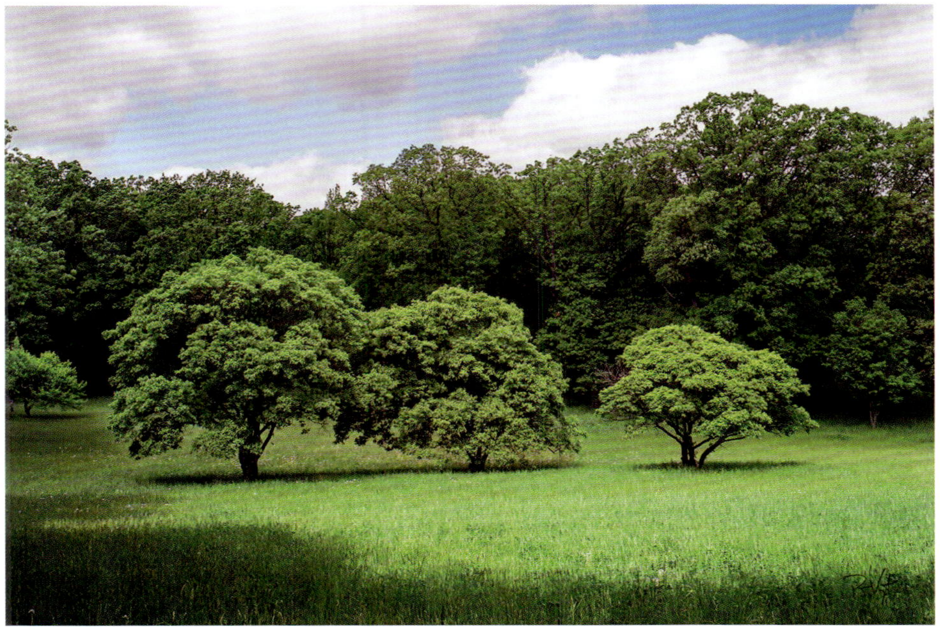

33. *Three Maple Trees, Summer 2005*

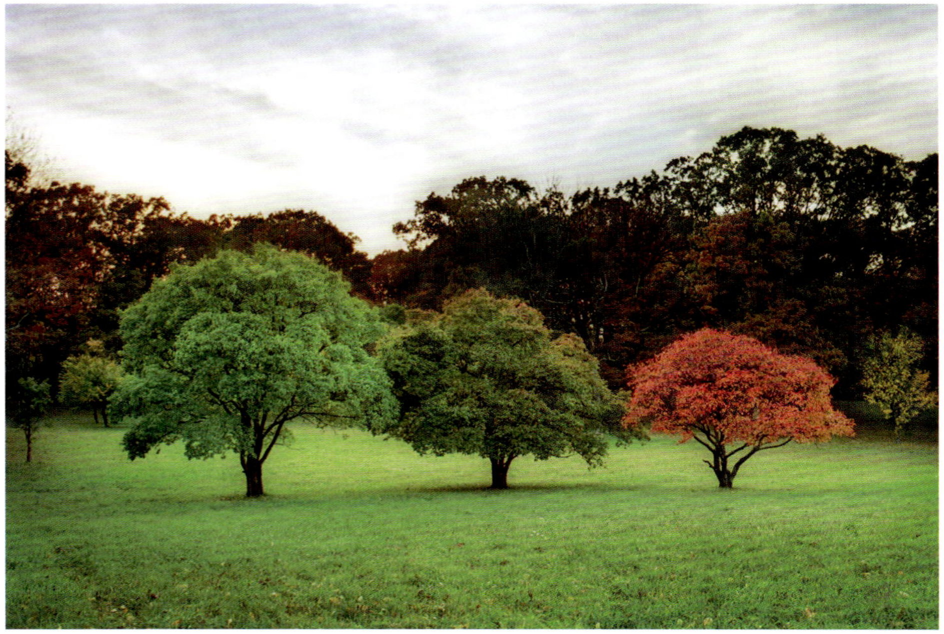

34. *Three Maple Trees, September 2005*

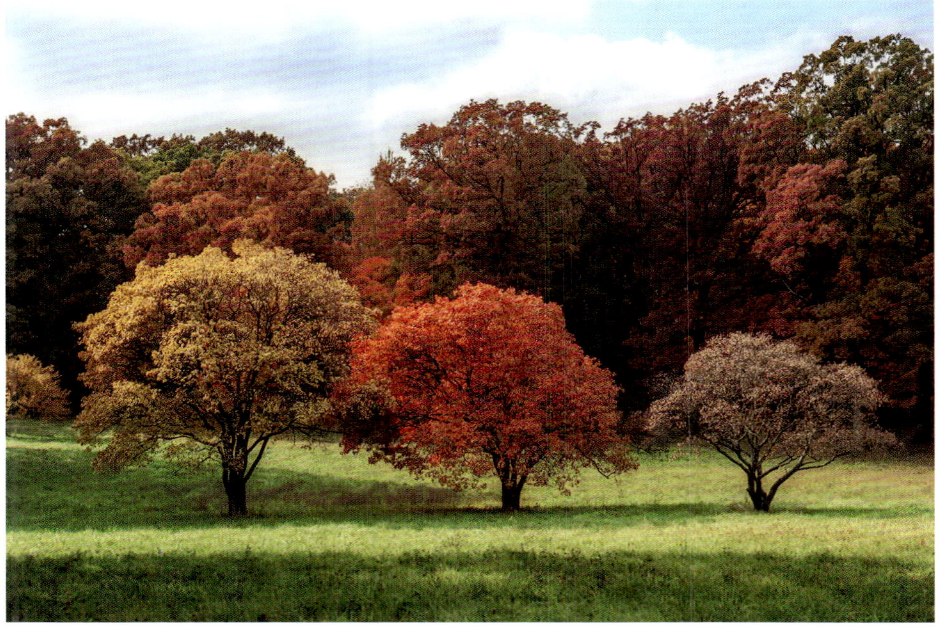

35. *Three Maple Trees, October 2003*

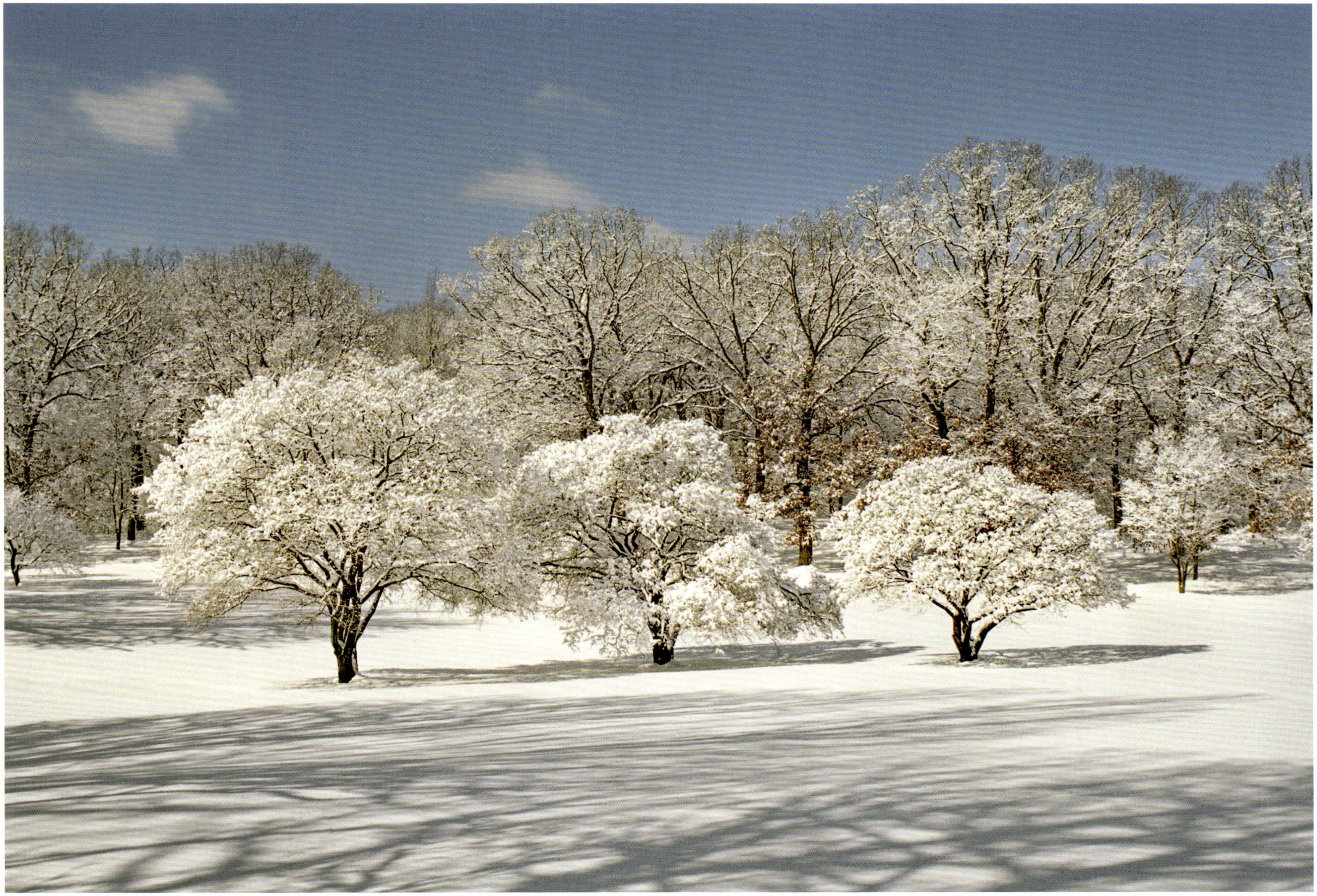

36. *Three Maple Trees in Winter, 2004*

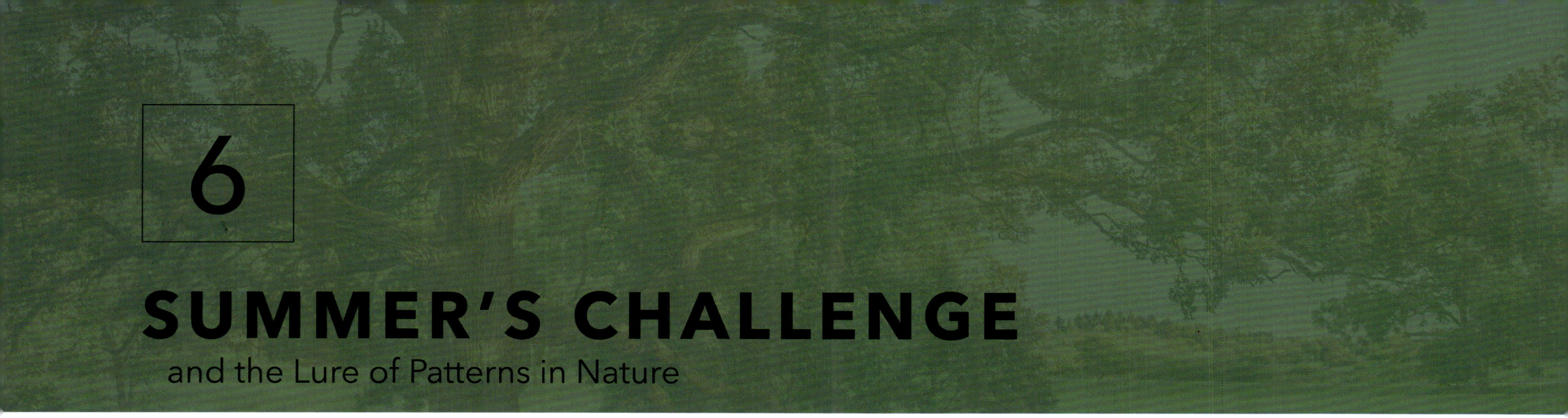

6

SUMMER'S CHALLENGE

and the Lure of Patterns in Nature

Spring, fall, and winter are tree bonanzas for finding pictures. Summer is tough. That's because our eyes love to see variations, delicate shapes, color contrasts, and lines that create paths for our imaginations to follow.

The challenge: In summer, big leafy trees are monochromatic (all green) and dense (their graceful branches hidden by summer leaves). I seek to overcome that challenge by either pulling back to get a wide encompassing view or by moving in and looking closely for patterns. I took the wider view to photograph the *Three Maples* series (Plates 32-36). The summer view (Plate 33) is mostly green. Yet the wider view makes a picture, contrasting the rolling boundary lines along the tops of the big leafy maple trees against the slightly darker background trees, then the line between cloud and blue sky echoes the rolling shape again.

There is also a challenge in looking close to find delicate and intricate patterns in nature, because patterns alone do not make a picture. *Robb's Almond Spurge* (Plate 37) comes close to being a "keeper" picture. I took it on an August morning after a light misty rain. I love the intriguing pattern built up in the smooth, shapely leaves and the complementary colors from rich emerald to silvery green. But it needs more. Patterns alone look merely "plaid." In this photograph, there's no circular song to enjoy. Was there a better picture to be taken of *Robb's Almond Spurge* that wet morning? Perhaps. But I don't know because I moved on after taking this photograph without engaging my feelings and seeking more.

The Morton Arboretum's Schulenberg Prairie is at its peak during the last half of June every summer. It is filled with beautiful flowers and intriguing patterns of stalk, branch, and tendril. The plants and patterns are all on a small scale, and I find it challenging to achieve anything beyond plaid in my photographs. It took several years and many June visits before, late on an overcast June day in 2006, I saw sunlight coming in low through a gap in the clouds at the horizon. The golden light skimmed across the grass while illuminating every blossom. I experienced a magical moment here and took some of it home with me in *Schulenberg Prairie at Sunset* (Plate 40.)

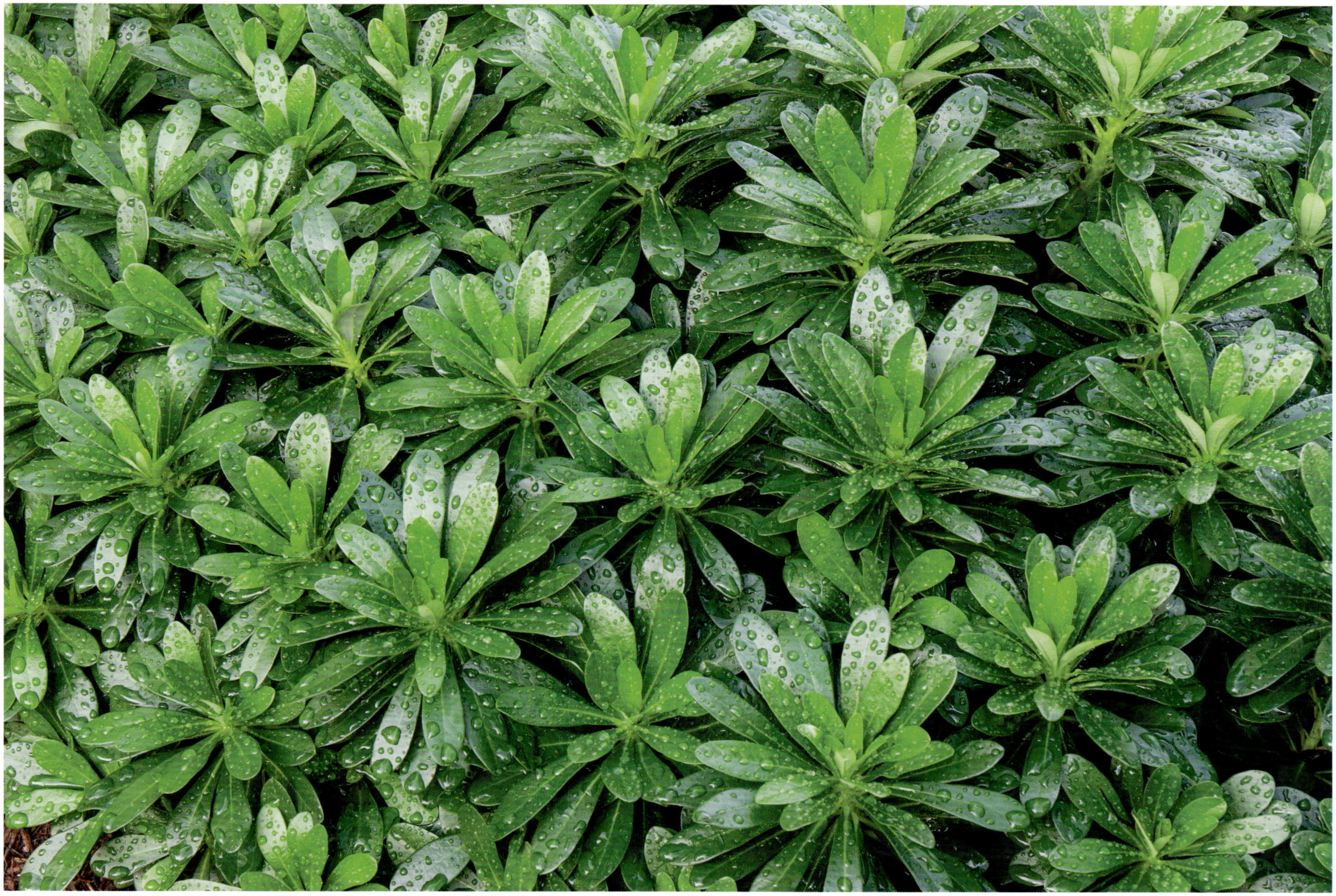

37. *Robb's Almond Spurge*, Ground Cover Garden, 2005

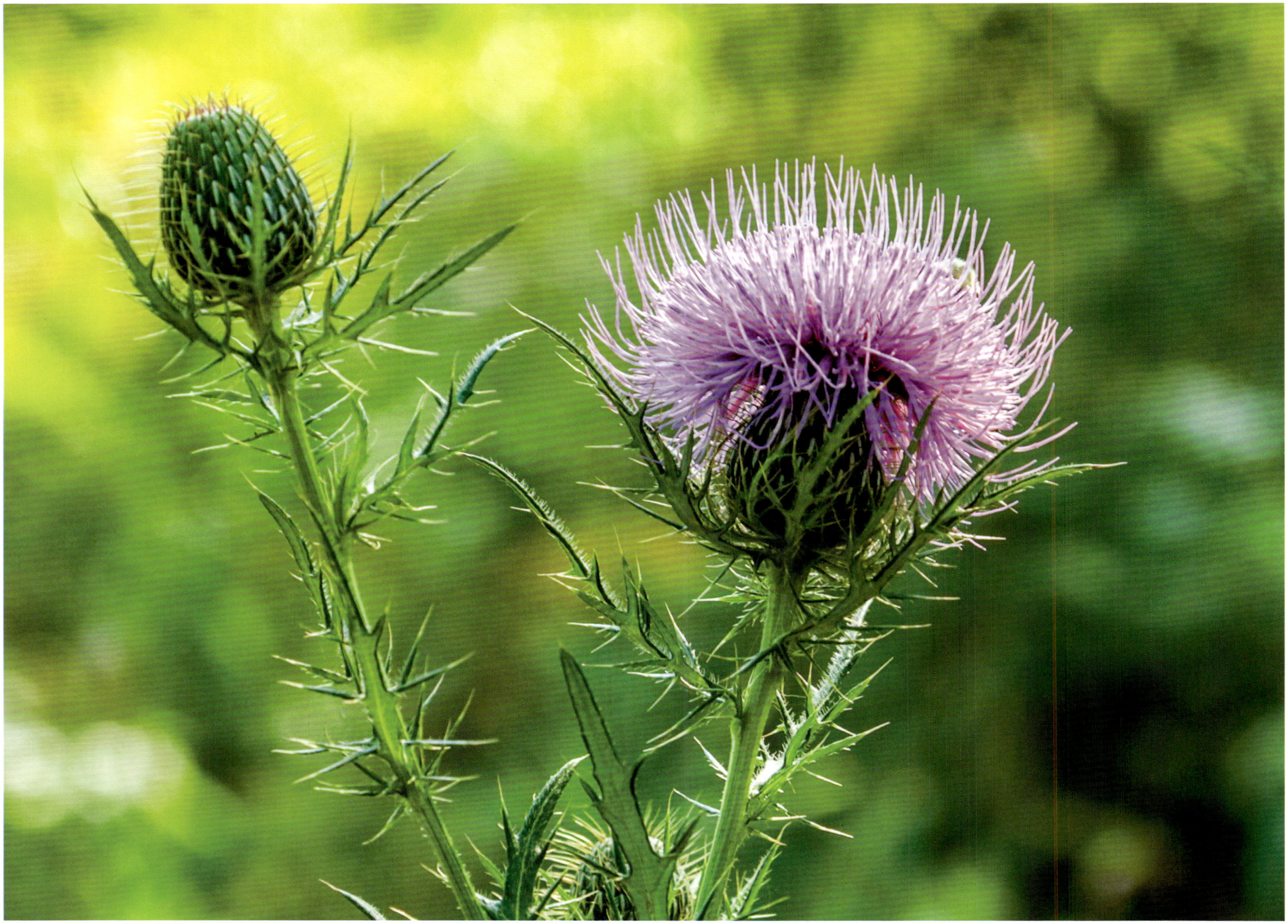

38. *Thistle Bud and Bloom*, near the Schulenberg Prairie, 2009
39. *Queen Anne's Lace beneath the Oaks*, 2014 (opposite)

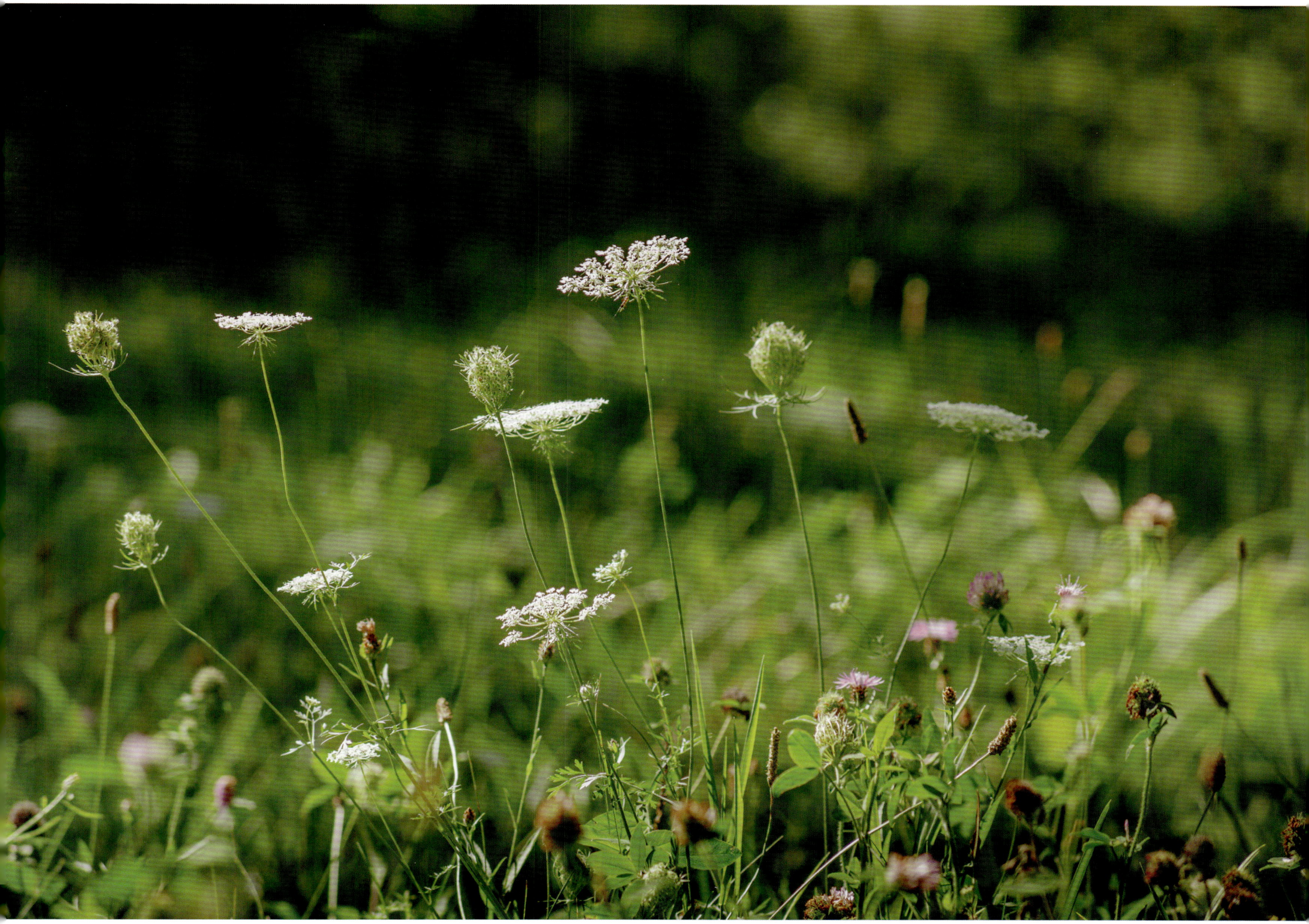

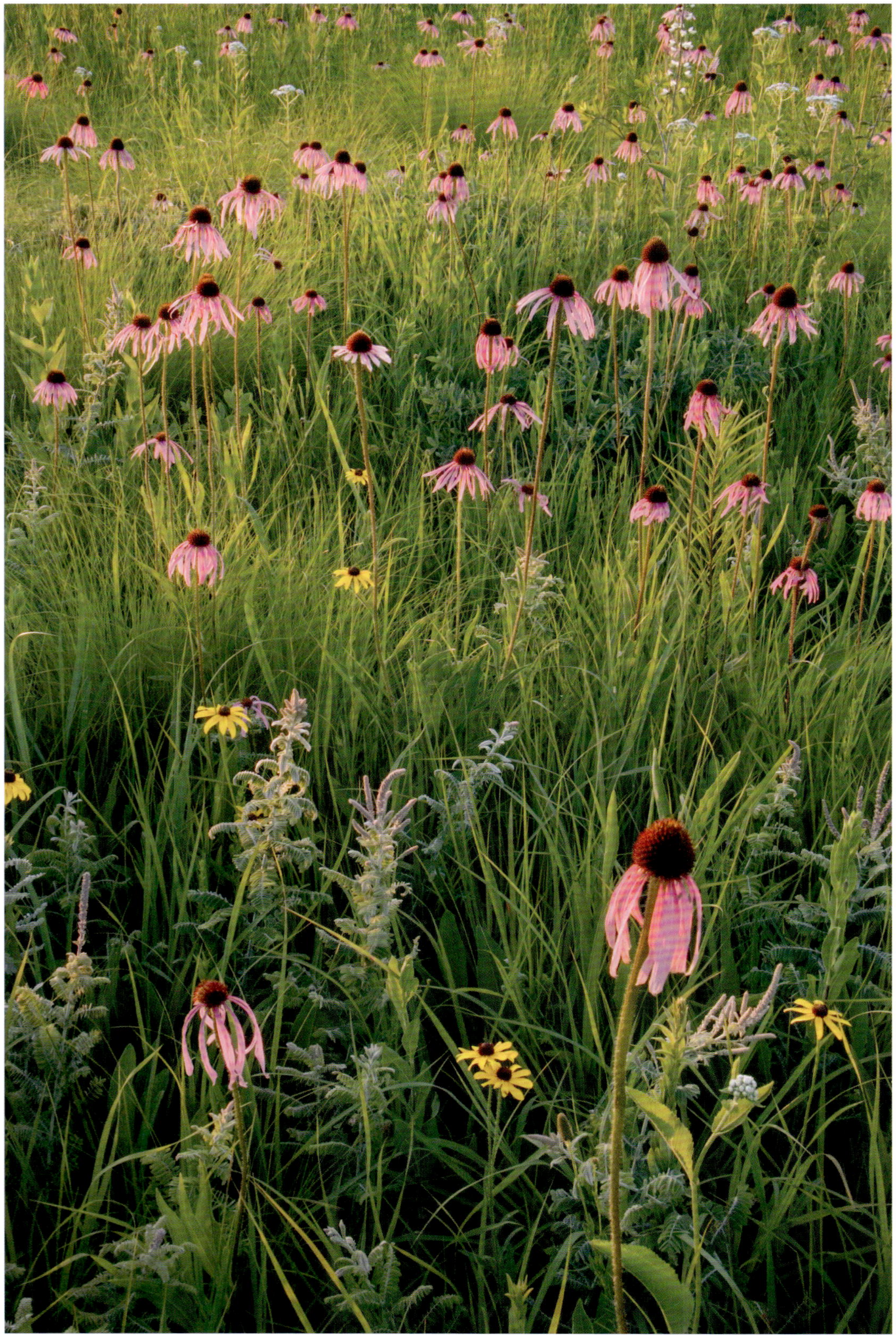

40. *Sunset at the Schulenberg Prairie*, 2006

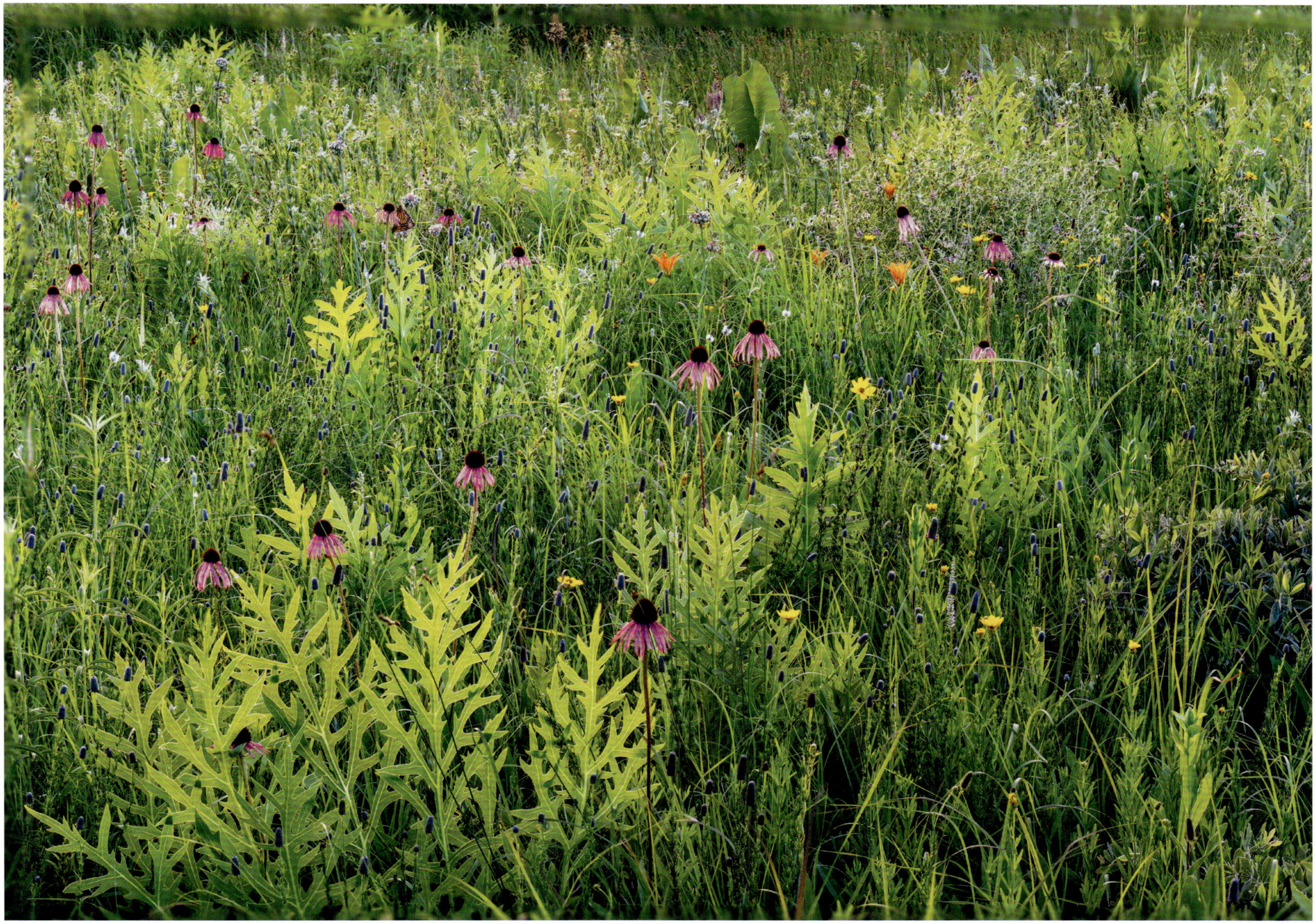

41. *Schulenberg Prairie in Bloom*, June 2018

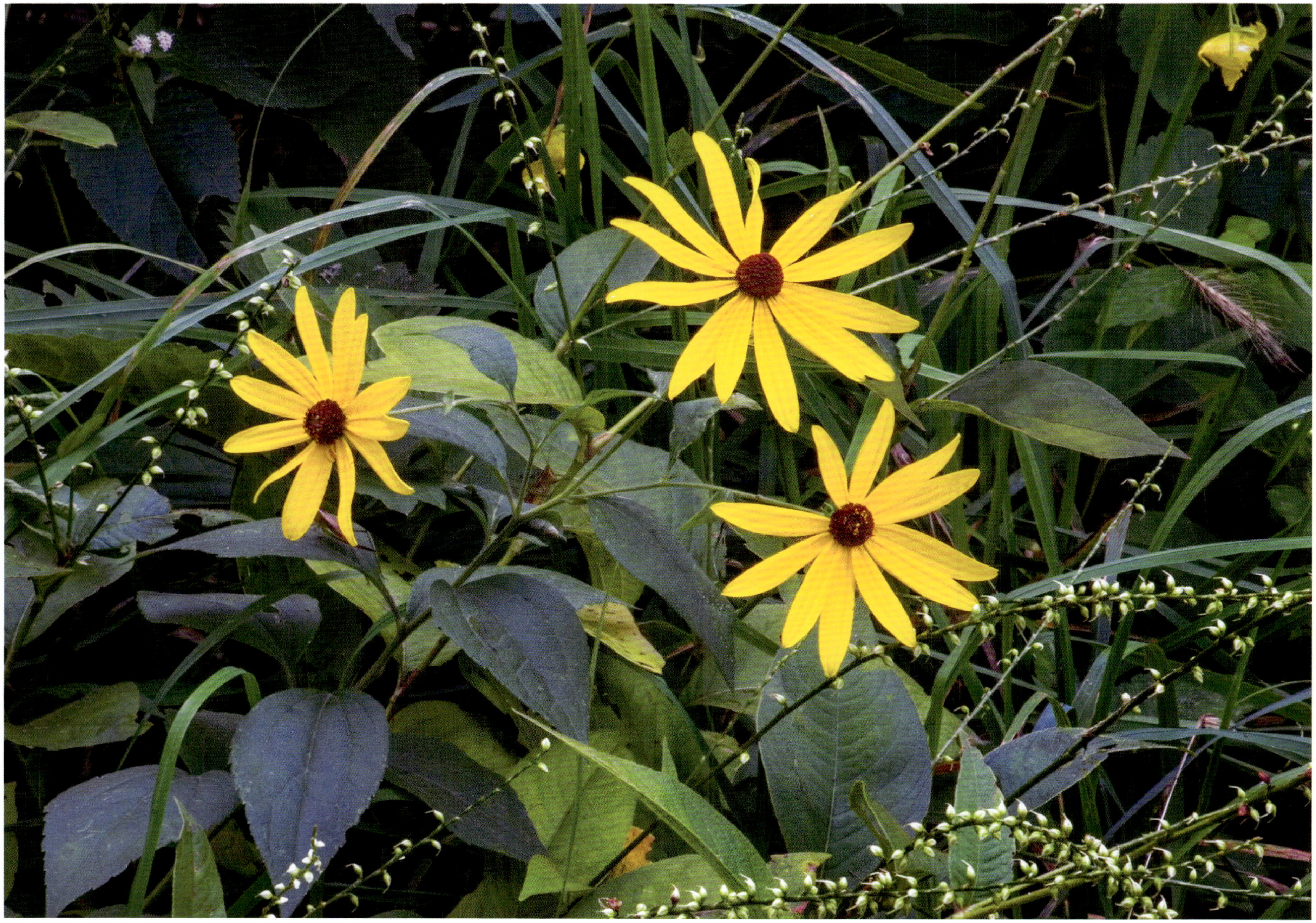

42. *Three Rudbeckia along Willoway Brook*, 2006

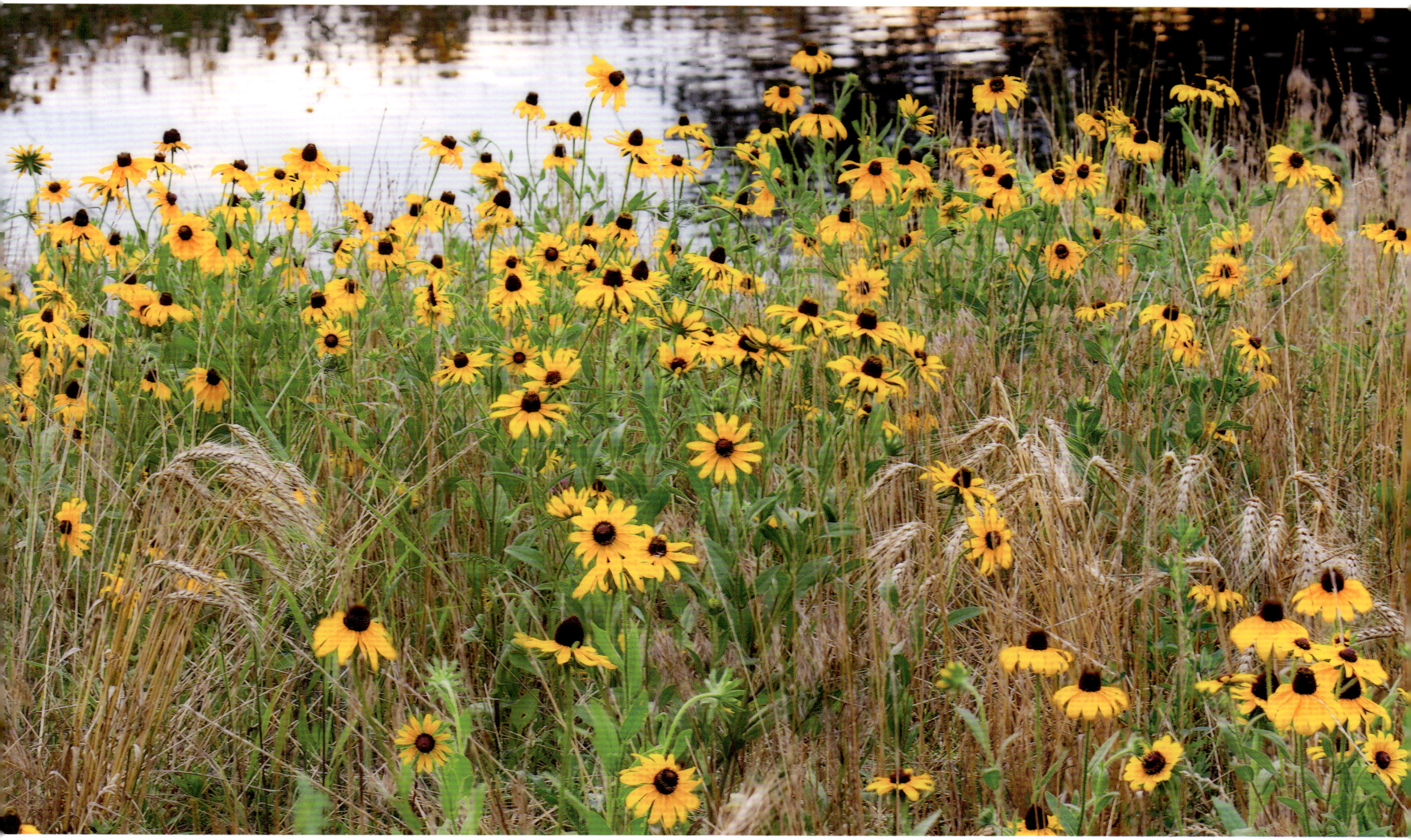

43. *Rudbeckia along the East Branch*, 2017

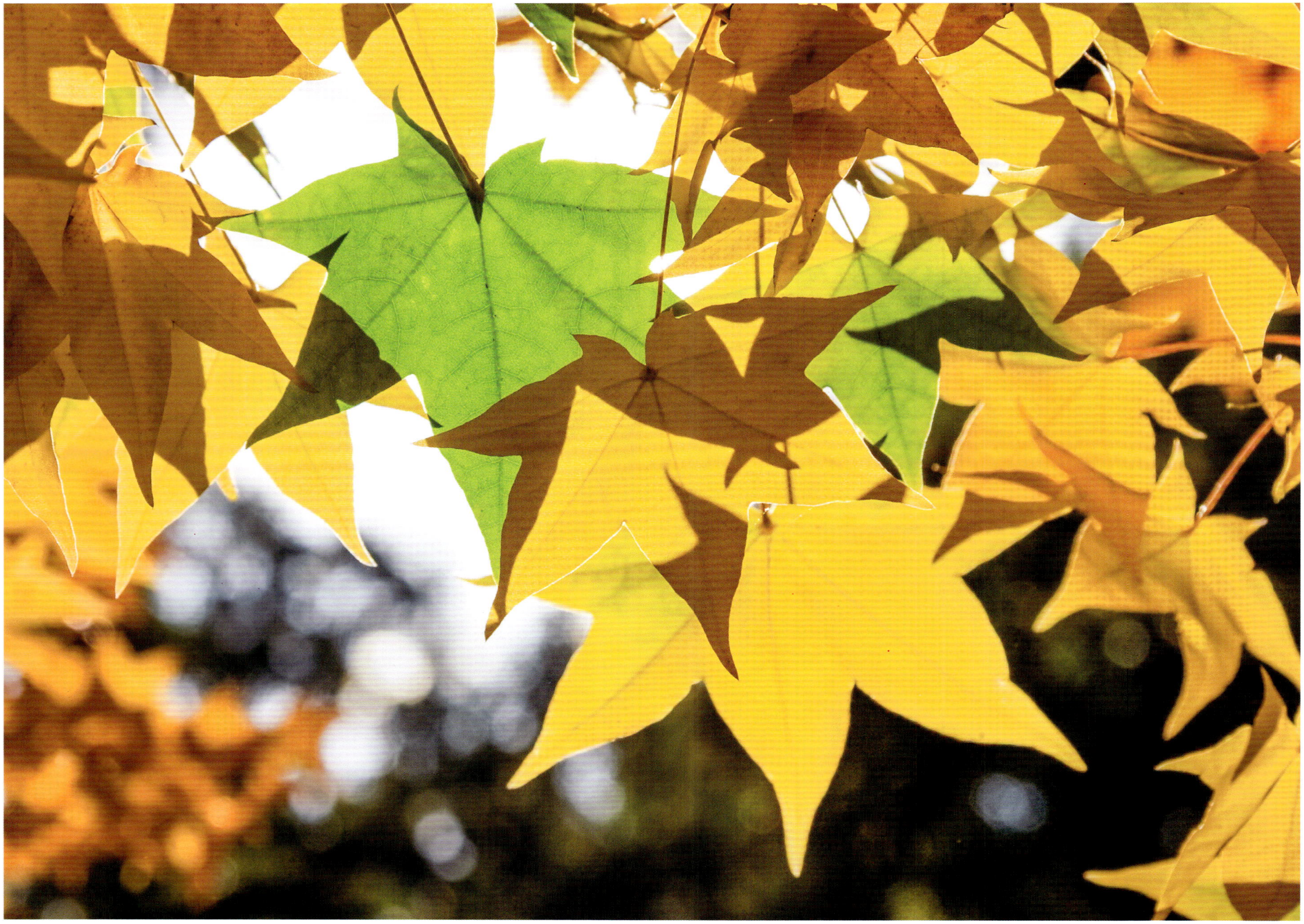

44. *Painted Maple Leaves*, East Side, 2008

7

FINDING PICTURES IN FALL

I love to walk in the woods when the air feels crisp and the leaves start to turn color. Who doesn't? It's not just the beautiful, changing colors. It's also the trees themselves. The shape and color of trees that have looked the same for four months are now changing every day. Just as in spring, in fall there are thousands of pictures we could take.

I have two very specific favorite and best times for finding pictures in fall: first colors (when the trees first begin to change colors) and last leaves (when only a few leaves remain on the trees). In mid-September most trees are still green, but each seems to be starting to exhibit a different green. After a week or two, half the leaves remain green, but the other half, still on the branches are orange and yellow (Plates 44, 57, and 58). Then when most of the leaves have fallen, usually by the first or second week of November, individual leaves and graceful branches are finally visible, and the colors tend to be deep orange and brilliant red (Plates 59, 60, and 62).

During these specific times, while walking at my favorite fall places, I often feel something stop me. I ask myself: "What am I seeing, right here? What's in front of me that's leading me to stop? Or what did I just pass by?"

The answer might be a curving branch loaded with red leaves. It might be a few leaves together, or it might be how the sun is finding its way to light up a single leaf. In 2005, a few crimson leaves grabbed my attention (Plate 45). On another day that same year, I saw one Schlesinger maple leaf that seemed to tell me the whole story of fall, all on its own (Plate 47). And in early November 2001, as I walked along a path, I was startled and then stopped by the incredible contrast in the color of three different maple trees. All the leaves on the far-right tree were still bright green (even though it was November); the leaves on the maple in the middle had turned bright yellow; and the leaves on the tree closest to me had all turned bright red. I'd never seen such a complete contrast in color on trees still so full of leaves (Plate 46).

45. *Sparkling Red Maple Leaf*, 2005

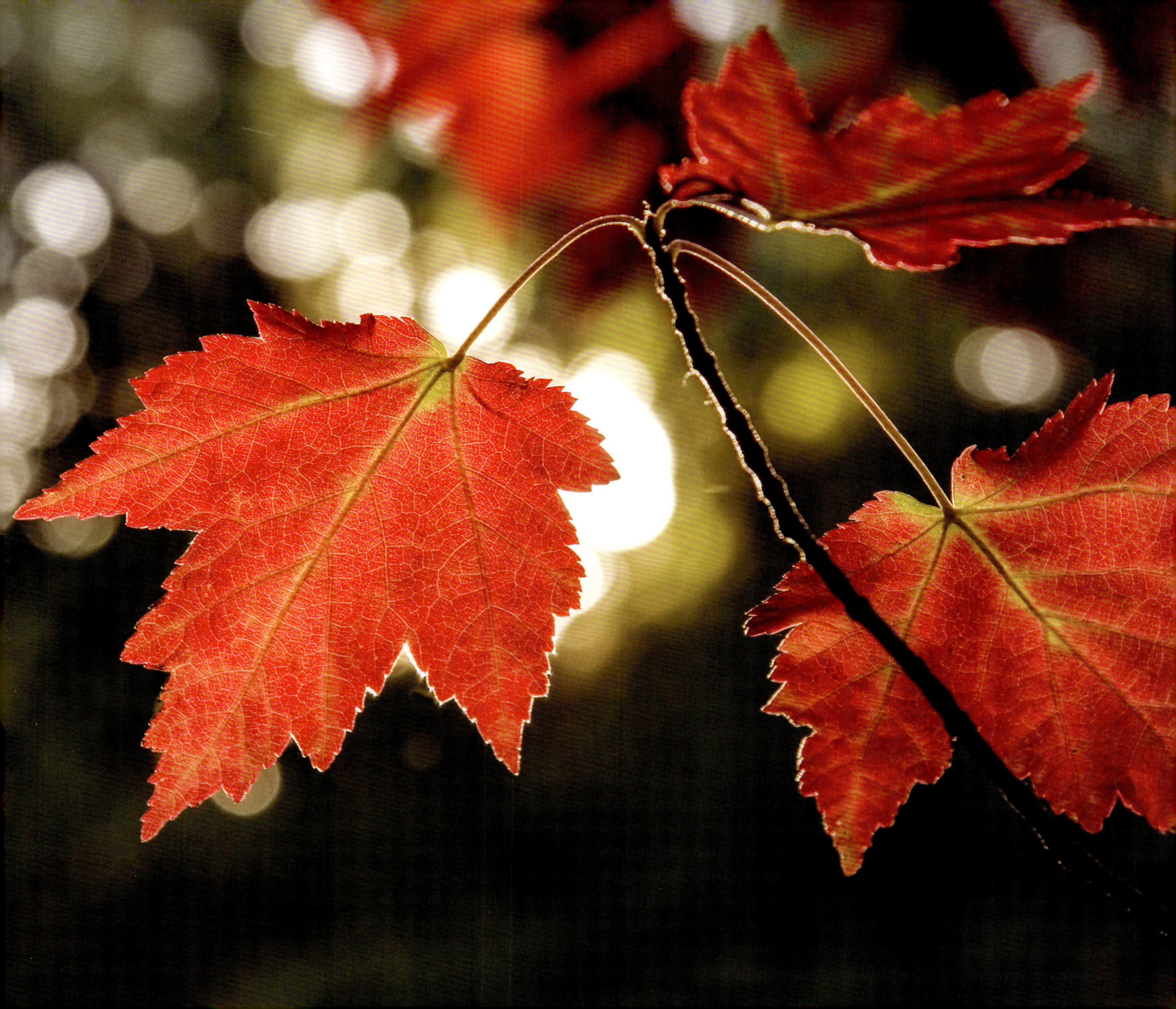

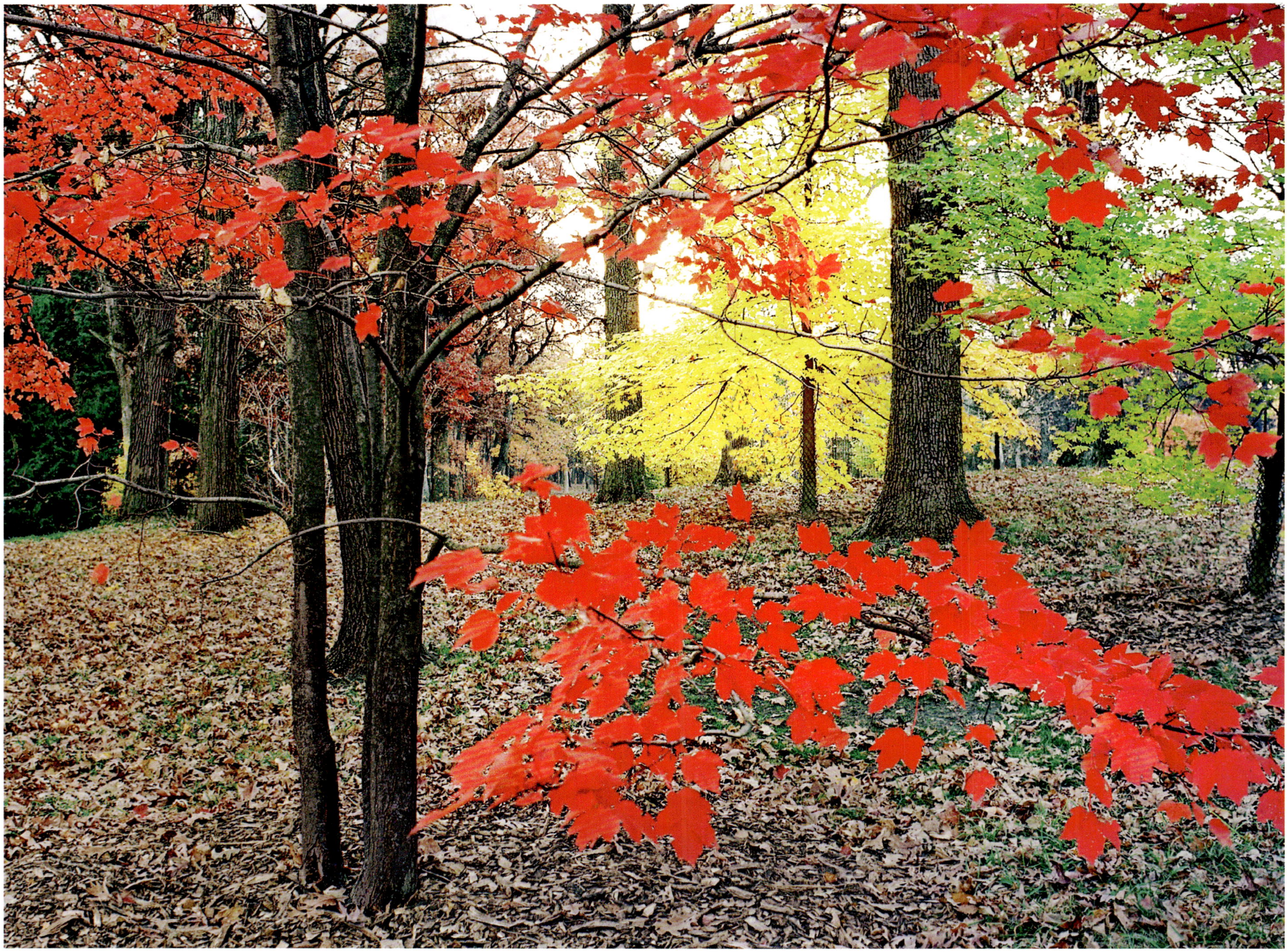

46. *Maple Collection*, near Parking Area P18, 2001

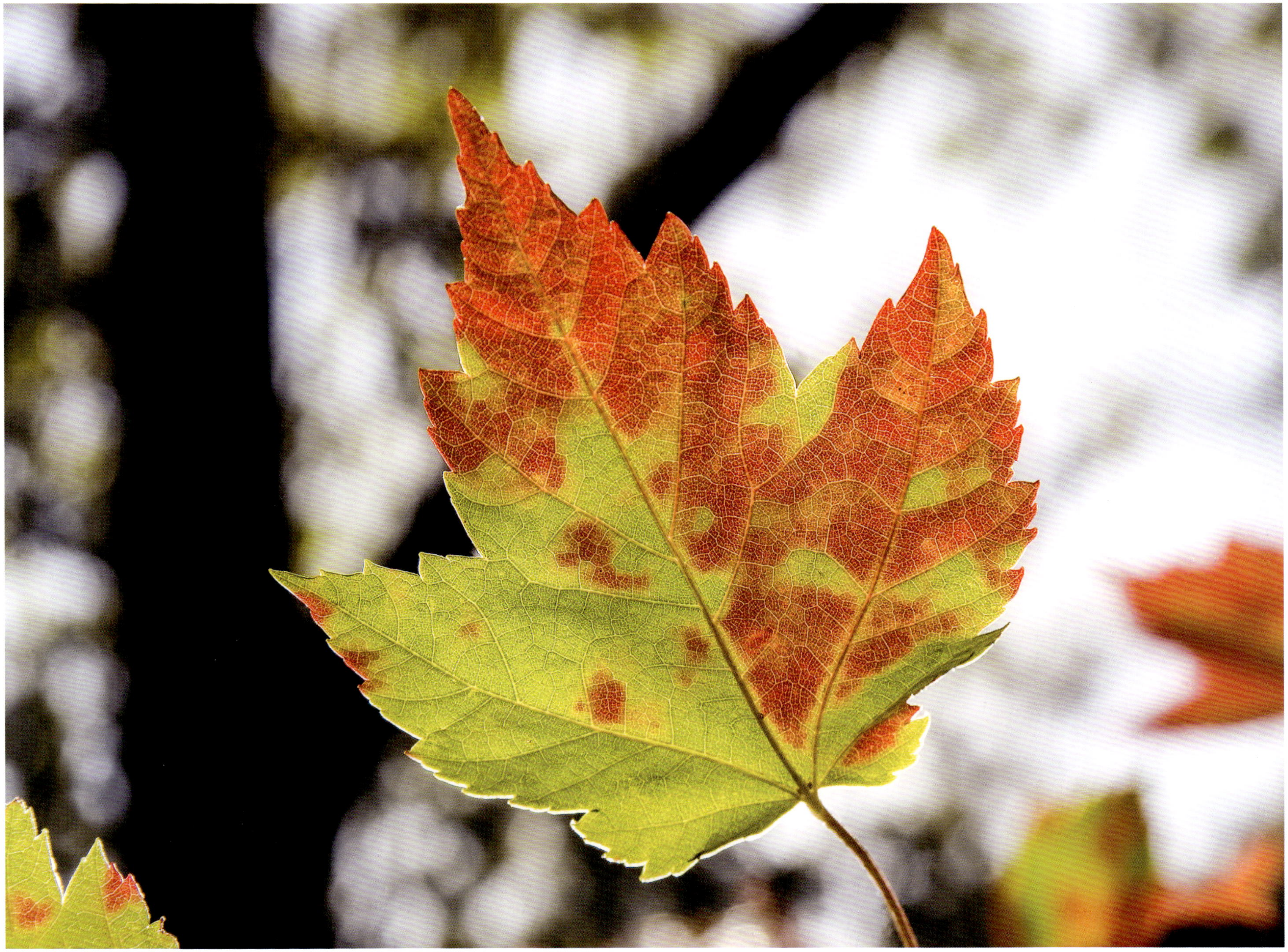

47. *Schlesinger Maple Leaf*, 2005

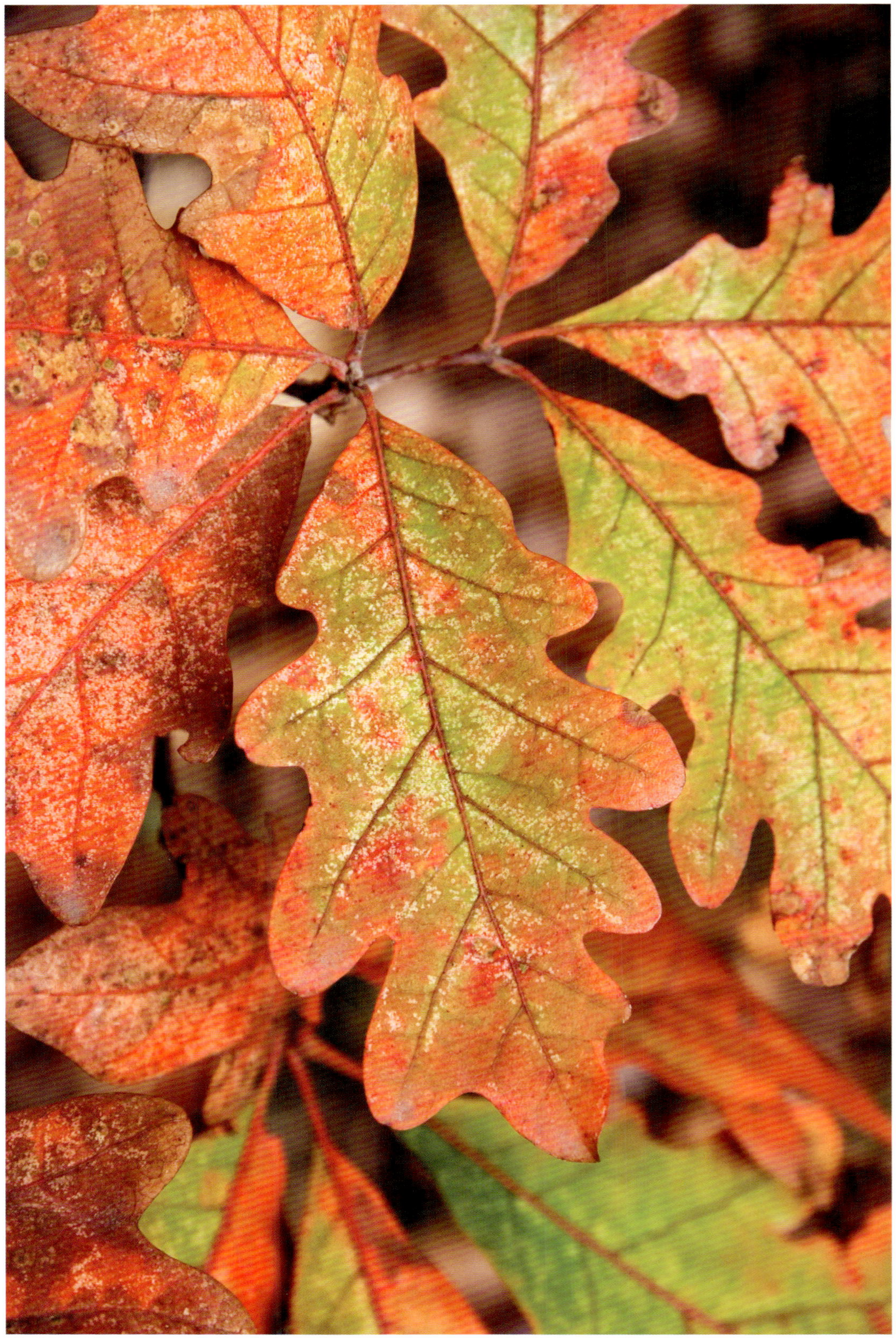

48. *Oak Leaves*, Morton Family Plot, 2005

49. *Fallen Leaves*, in the Maple Glade, 2009 (opposite)

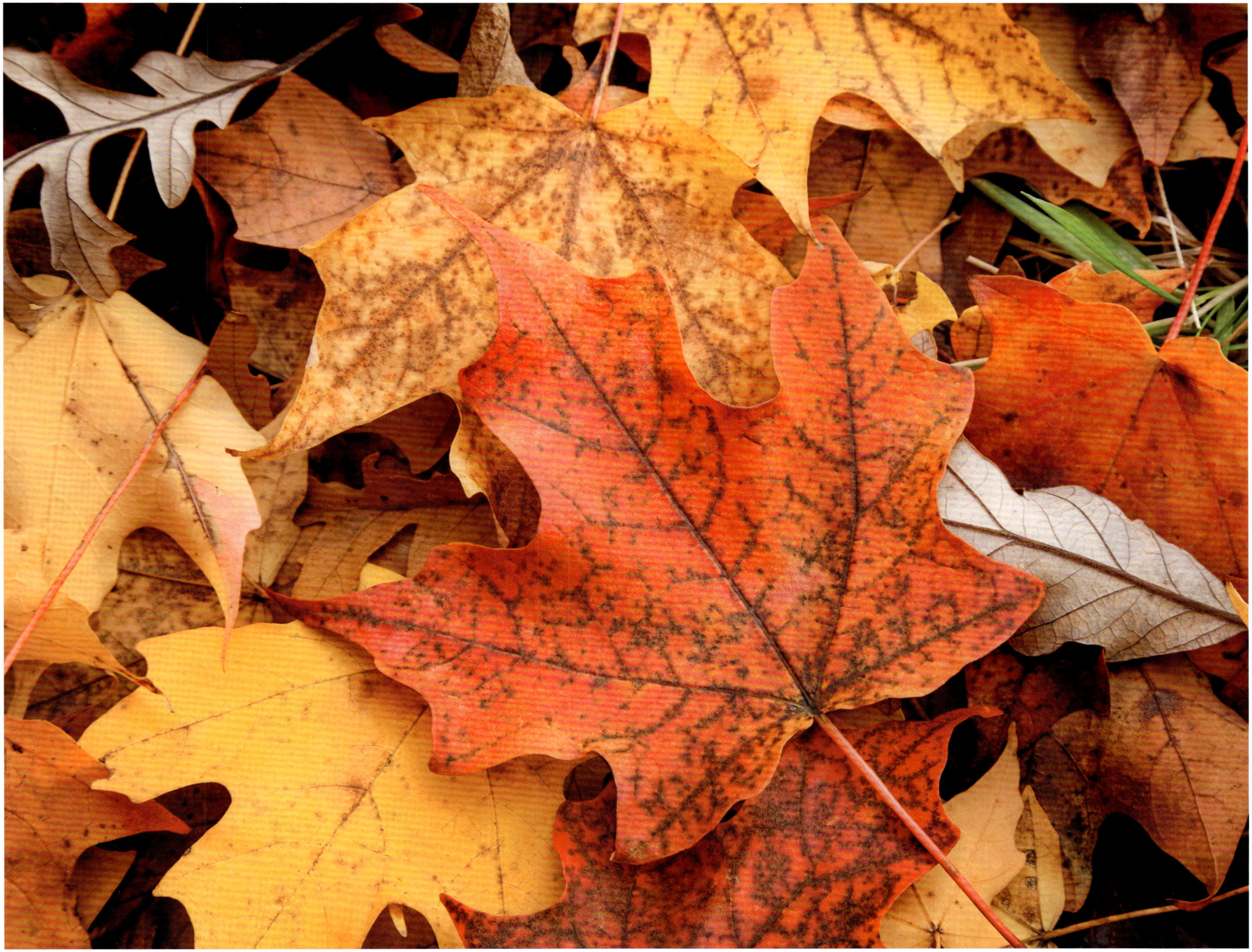

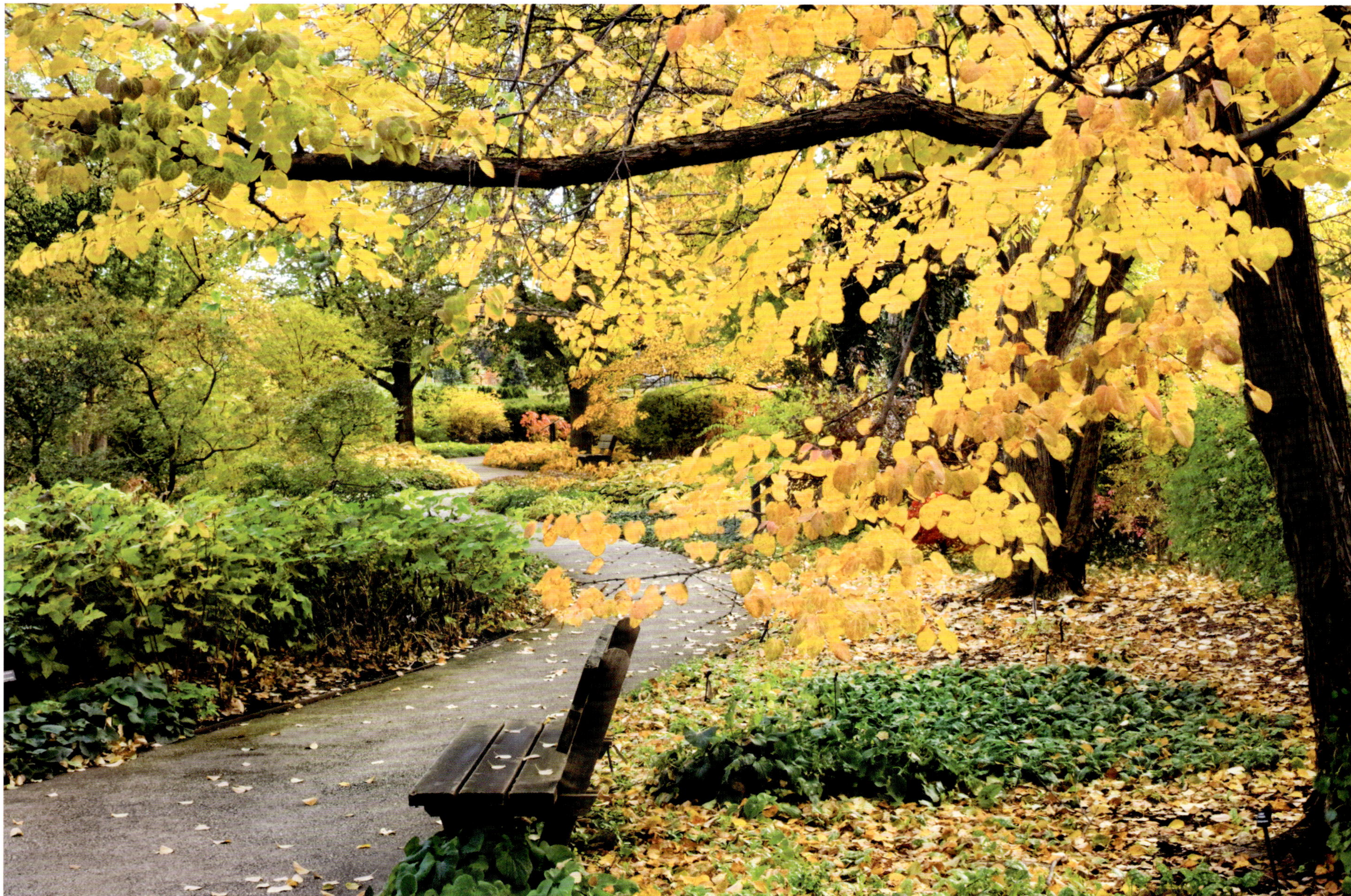

50. *Katsura Tree*, in the Ground Cover Garden, 2006

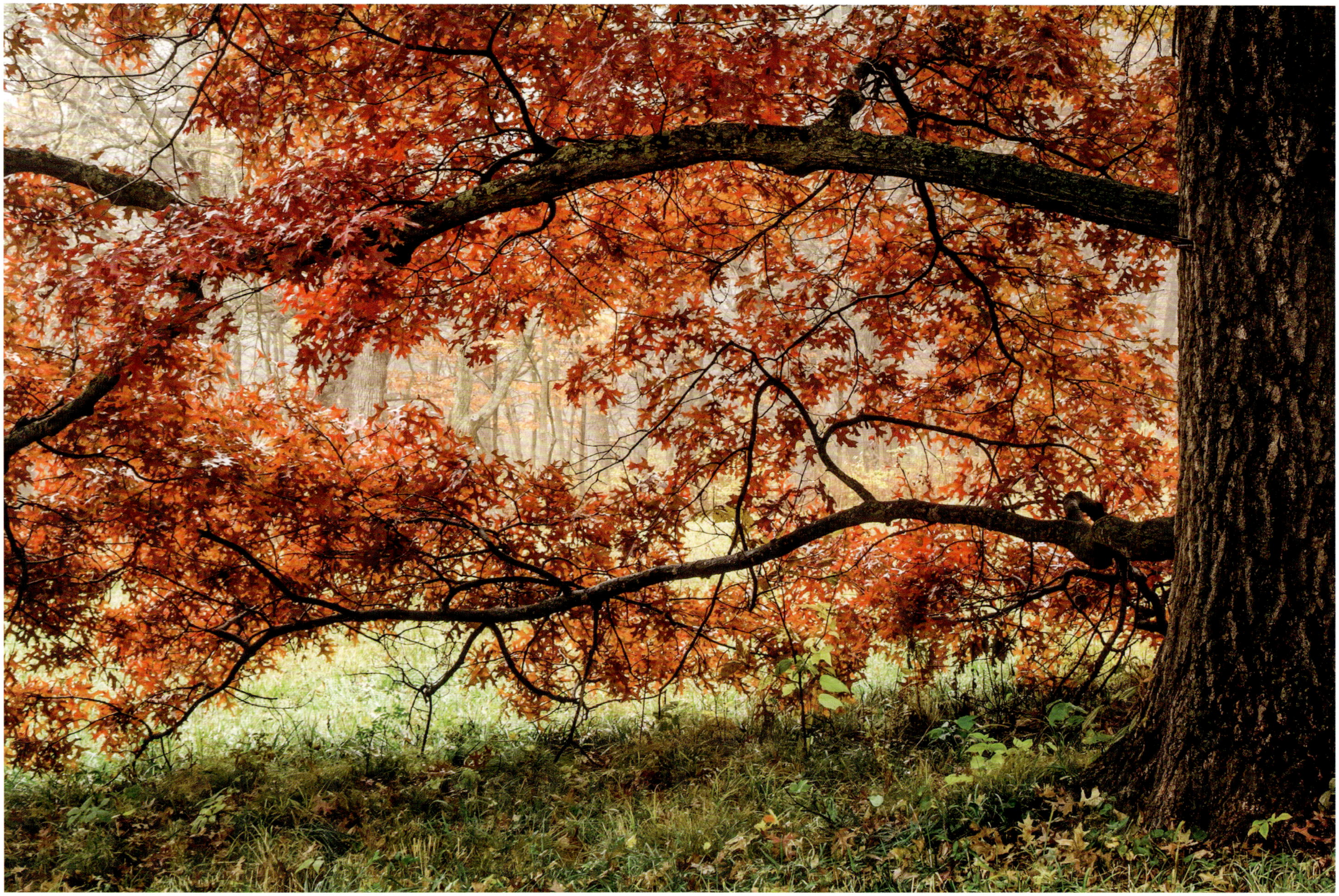

51. *Red Oak Branches on a Misty Morning*, near Parking Area P27, 2015

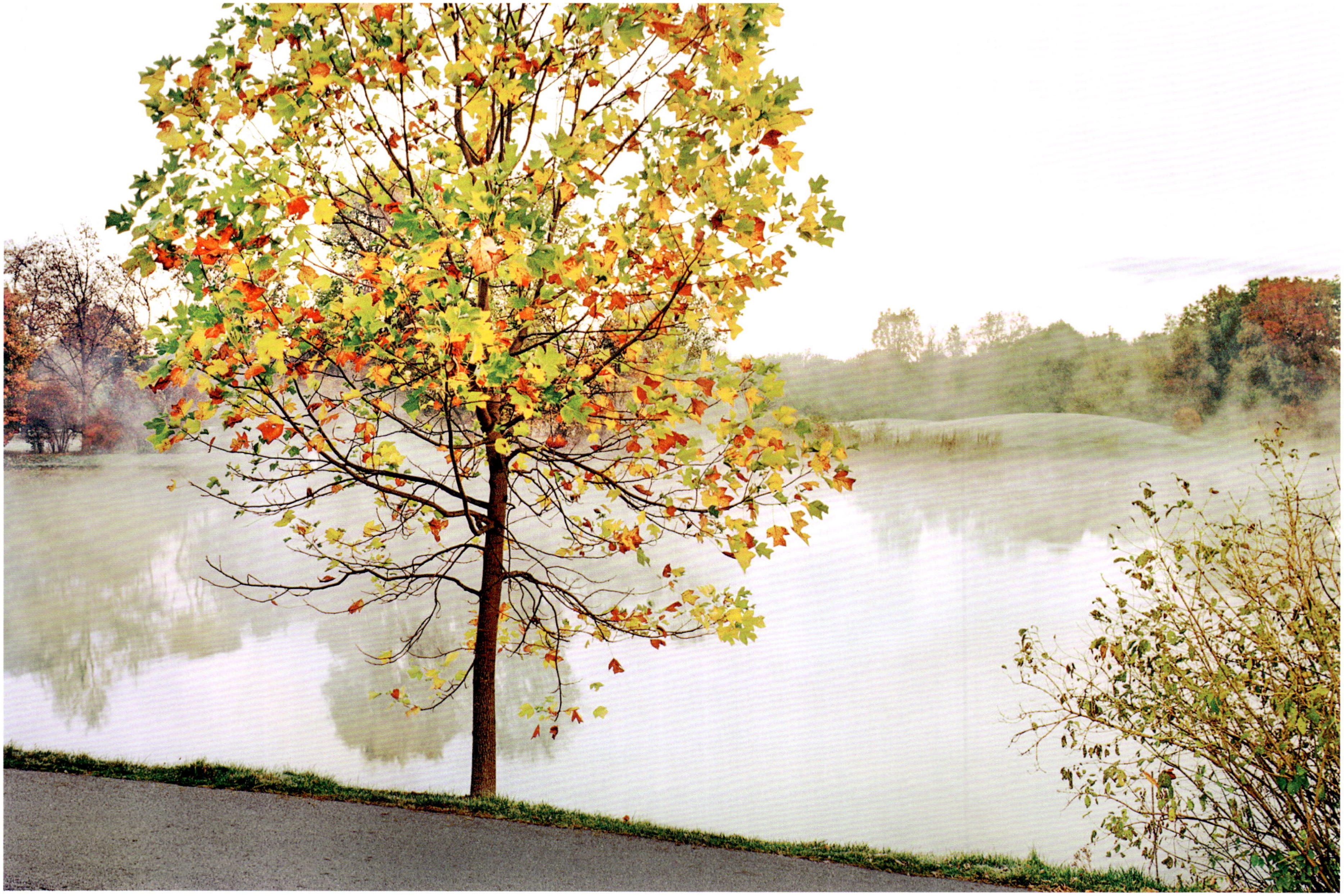

52. *Tulip Tree on the Shore of Old Meadow Lake*, 2000

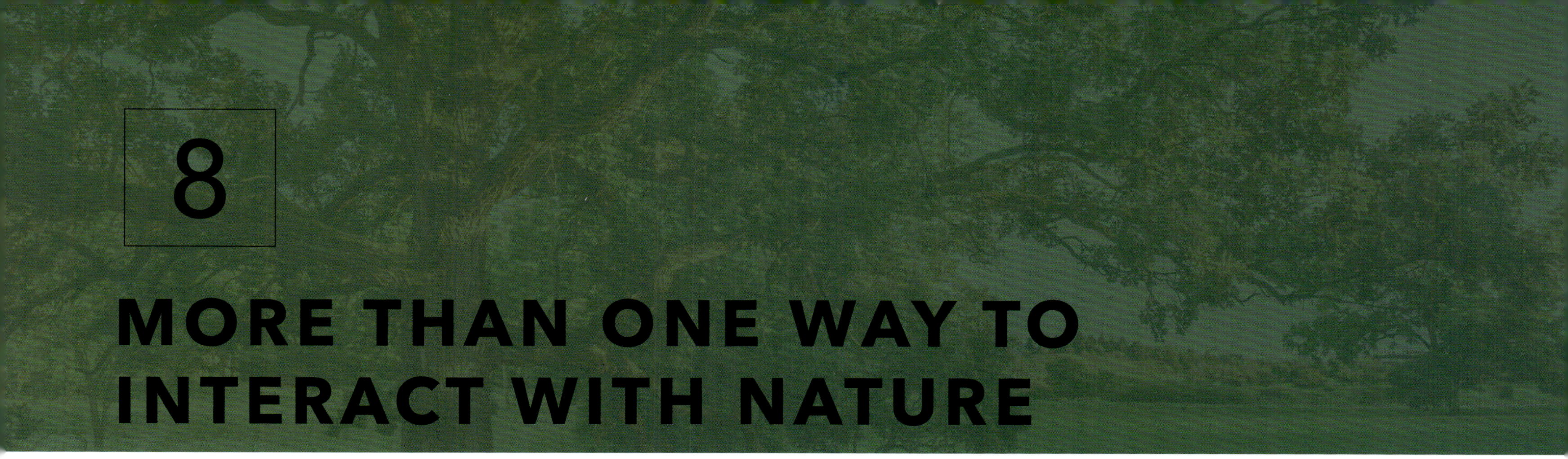

8

MORE THAN ONE WAY TO INTERACT WITH NATURE

Walking in the woods and seeing trees helps me regain balance and peace in my life, most of the time. But sometimes I go outdoors because I'm looking for some excitement, a challenge, a spark of inspiration. We don't need to go to the Rockies, Yosemite, or an ocean for either. Restorative calm is available in any meadow. Excitement and challenge are available in any stand of trees we visit. We can rest in a scene by physically stepping back from it. Or we can aggressively interact with a scene by physically stepping into it, towards it.

In section three (Page 14), I explained that the primary actions I can take to change the arrangement of lines, shapes, and colors in my camera are to change the place or time of the photograph. There is a third action I can take. That is to change the focal length of the camera by zooming in or zooming out (or by changing lenses). You might think that I zoom in to make leaves, branches, and trees look closer; likewise, you might think that I zoom the lens out to get a wider view, to fit more leaves, flowers, or trees into a picture. But I can accomplish those things by simply moving closer or moving further away. I don't need to zoom or to own extra lenses. The real power is that when I combine zooming out wider with moving closer, or I combine zooming in closer, with moving further away, I am changing the perspective of my view. Such a perspective change can change or emphasizes the mood of a picture.

The next two pictures have similar subject matter; both are beautiful trees in peak fall color. But they have different moods, which I emphasized by changing the lens that I used.

The first, *Yellow Maple* (Plate 53), is a quiet picture presenting an intricate design of curving branches, completely unsymmetrical yet comfortably balanced. I loved the calm, magisterial mood I felt in its presence. I was able to draw out the quiet, gentle patterns in *Yellow Maple* by first physically moving back thirty feet from the tree. Then I zoomed back in toward the tree with my lens. In doing so, the tree stayed about the same size on my screen, but I subtly emphasized the mood of calm tranquility.

I did the opposite for *Beech Splay* (Plate 54), a dynamic, exciting picture with a collection of angular lines, thrusting branches, and flurries of colors. To take this picture, I walked in close until I was almost touching the nearest branch. Then, I zoomed the camera back out (with a wide-angle lens), so the tree looked further away from me than it actually was. The resulting perspective change exaggerates the distances within the tree and increases the angles of the branches, adding to the picture the energy and drama I felt when I saw this tree.

Other wide-angle photographs (step in close and zoomed out) are *Daffodils Circling Redbud Trees* (Plate 4), *Maple Collection* (Plate 46), and *Oak Trees in Late October* (Plate 56). Note the immediacy and energy they project.

Examples of gently balanced, less tension-filled pictures taken with a moderate telephoto lens (I moved away and zoom back in) include *Gallant Oaks in Light Rain* (Plate 14), *Schulenberg Prairie in Bloom* (Plate 41), and *Eleven Trees* (Plate 67).

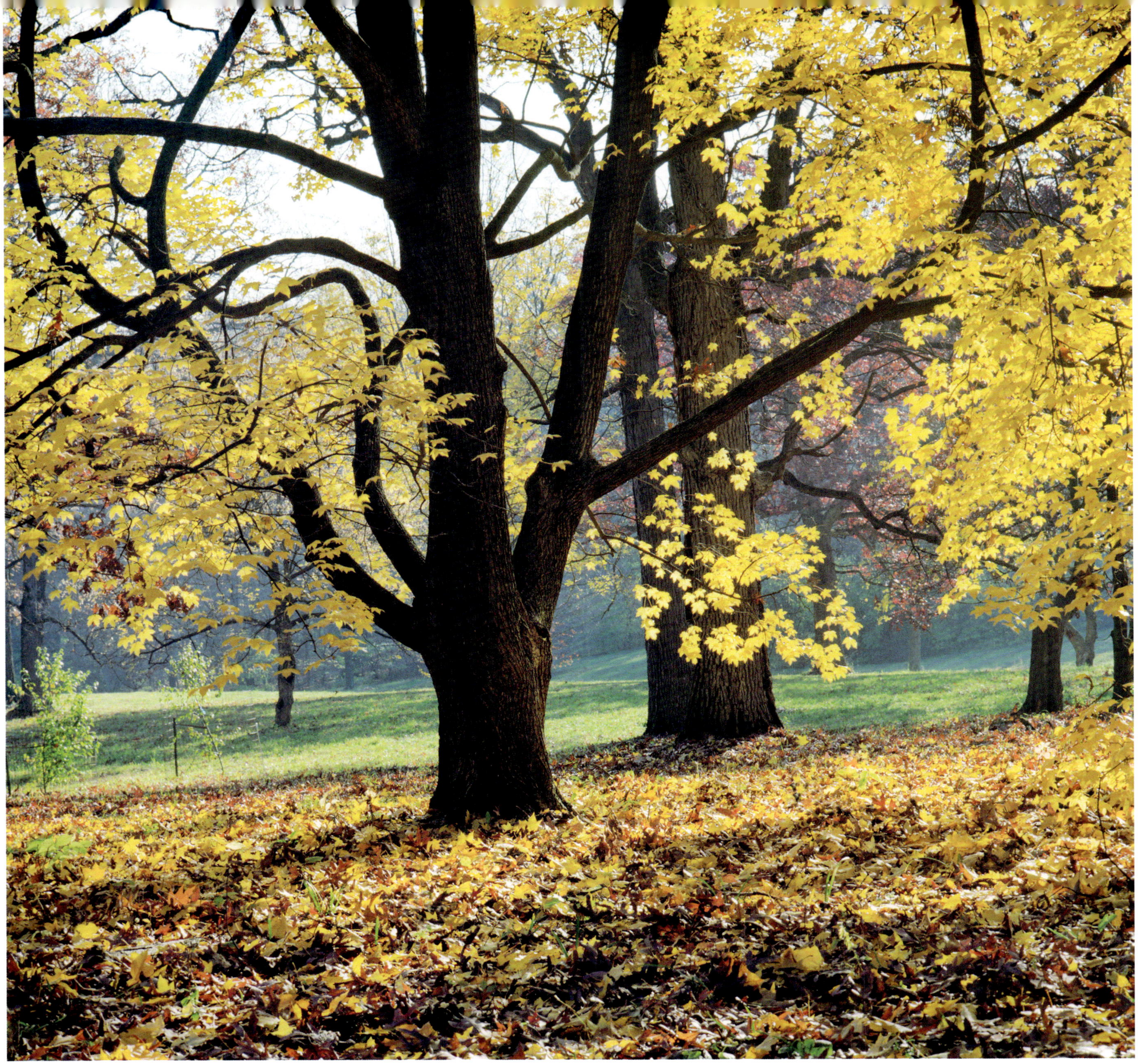

53. *Yellow Maple*, East Side, 2005

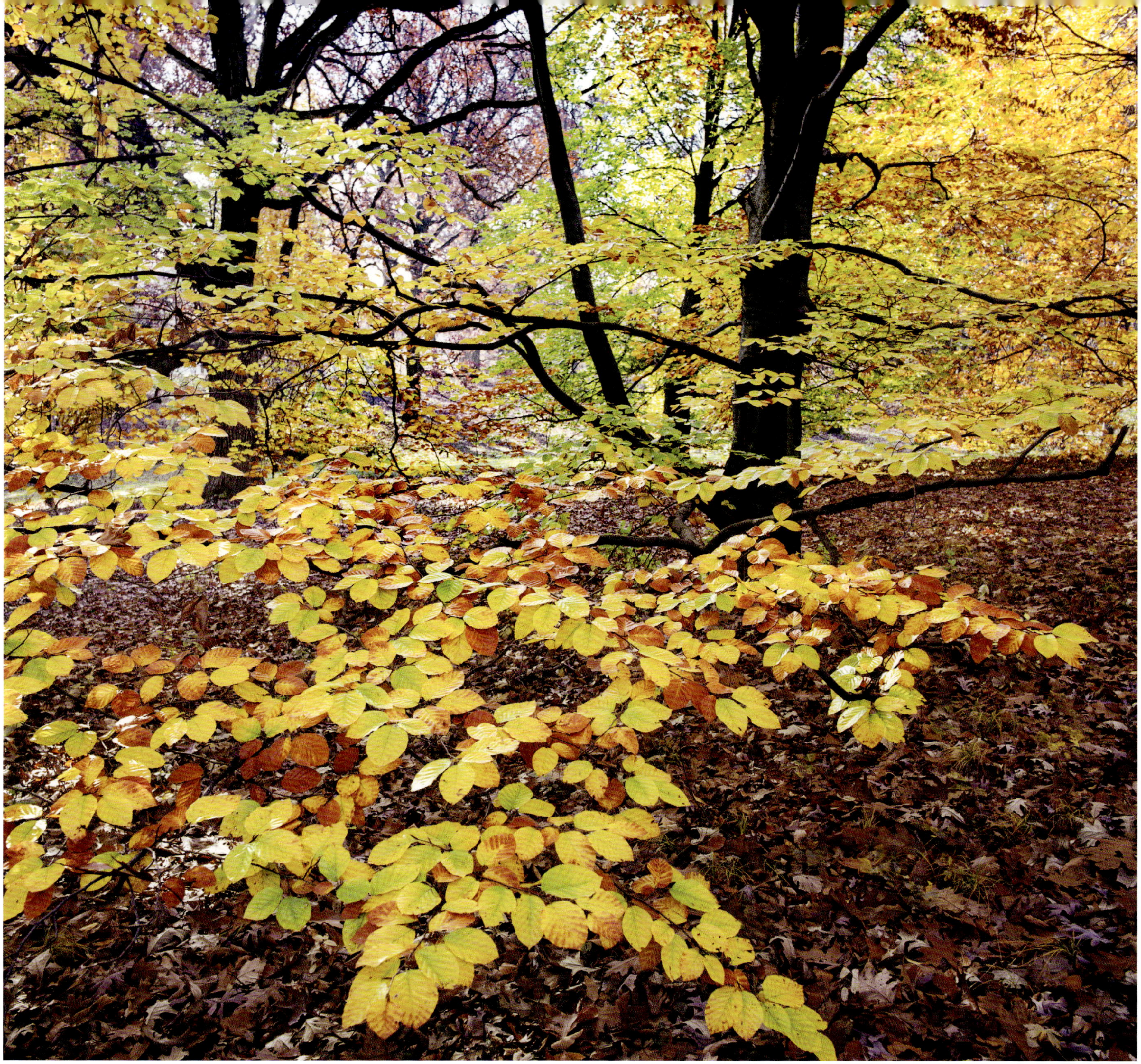

54. *Beech Splay*, near Parking Area P14, 2005

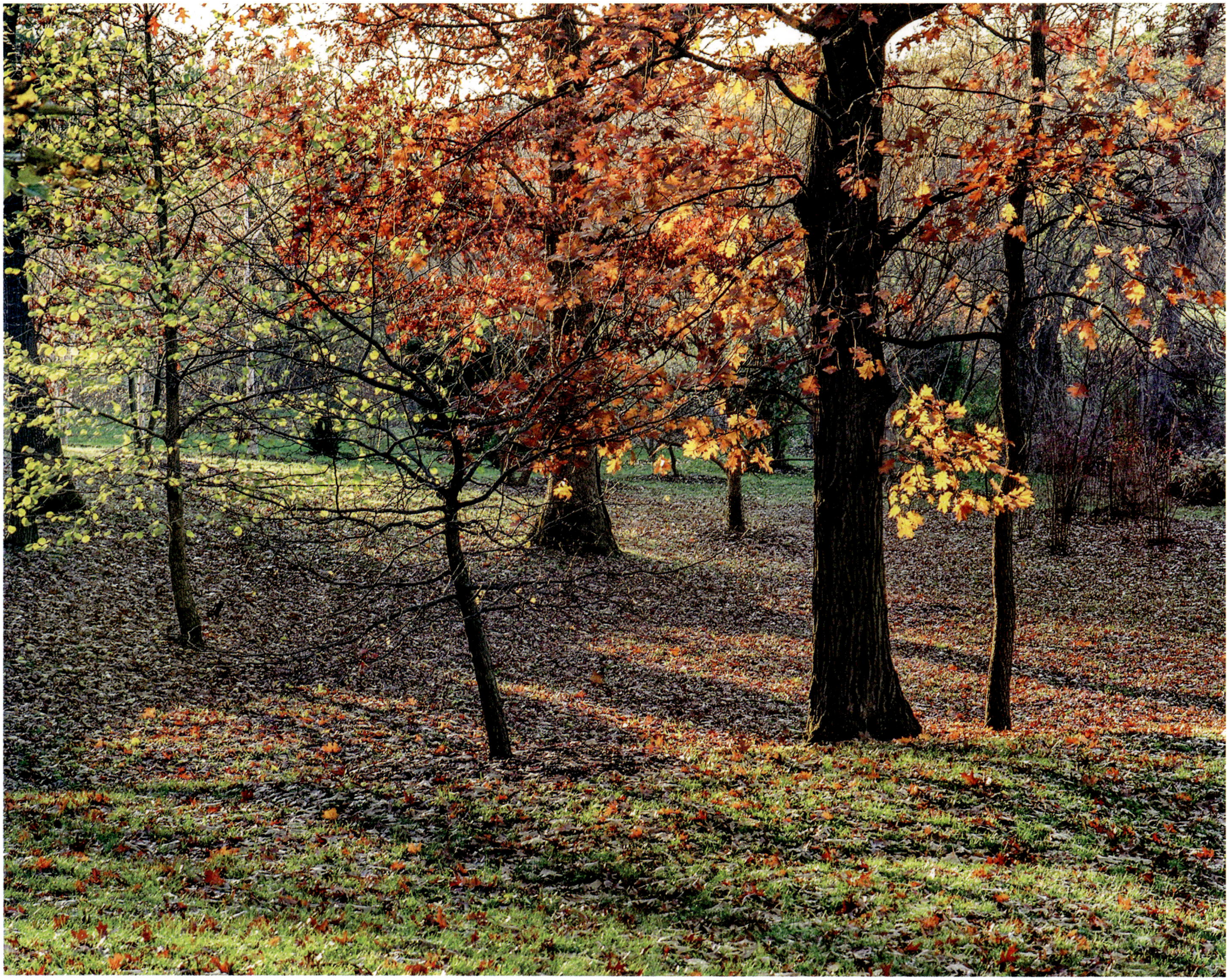

55. *Evening Sun across the Appalachian Collection*, East Side, 2005

56. *Oak Trees in Late October*, 2015 (opposite)

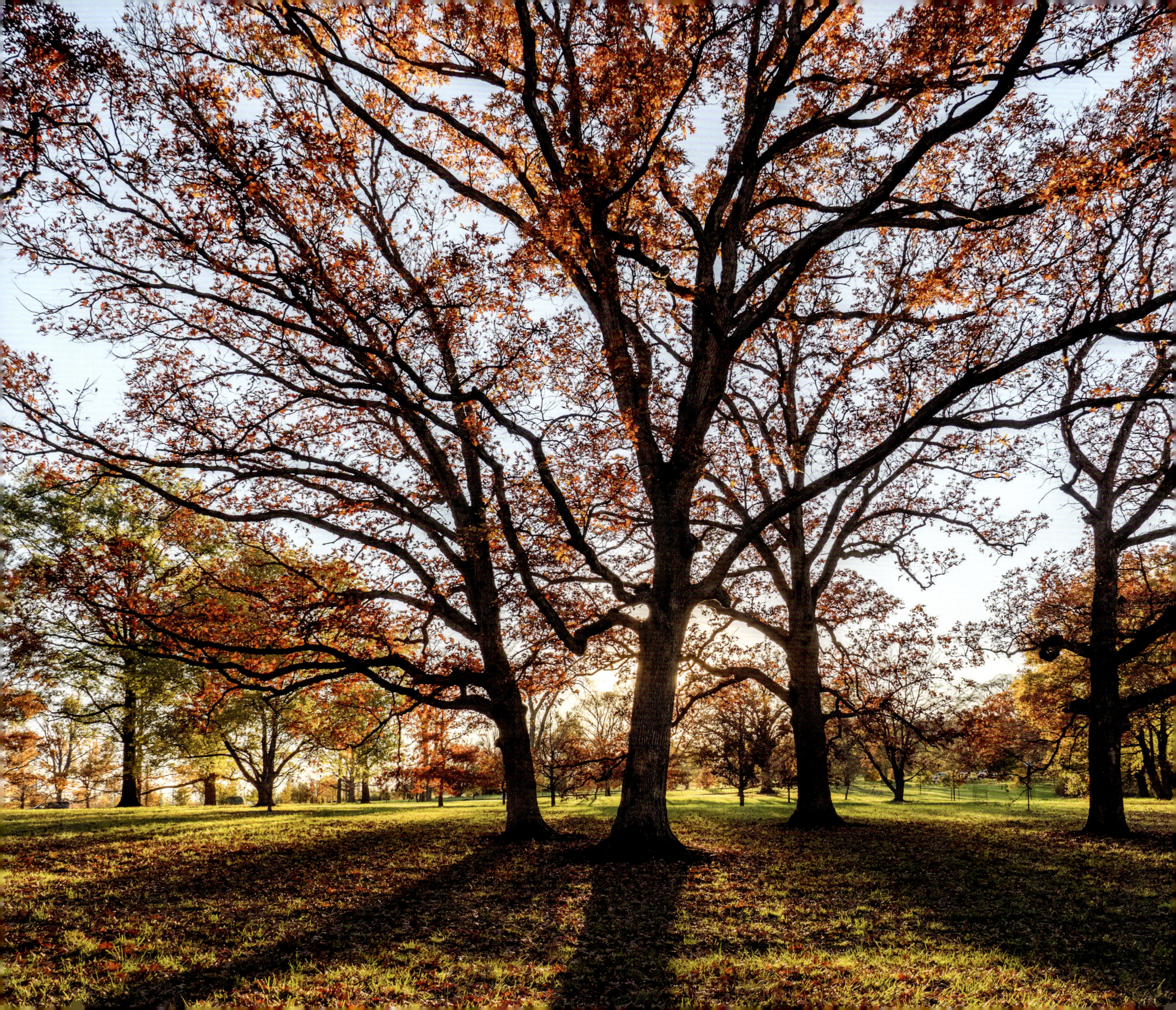

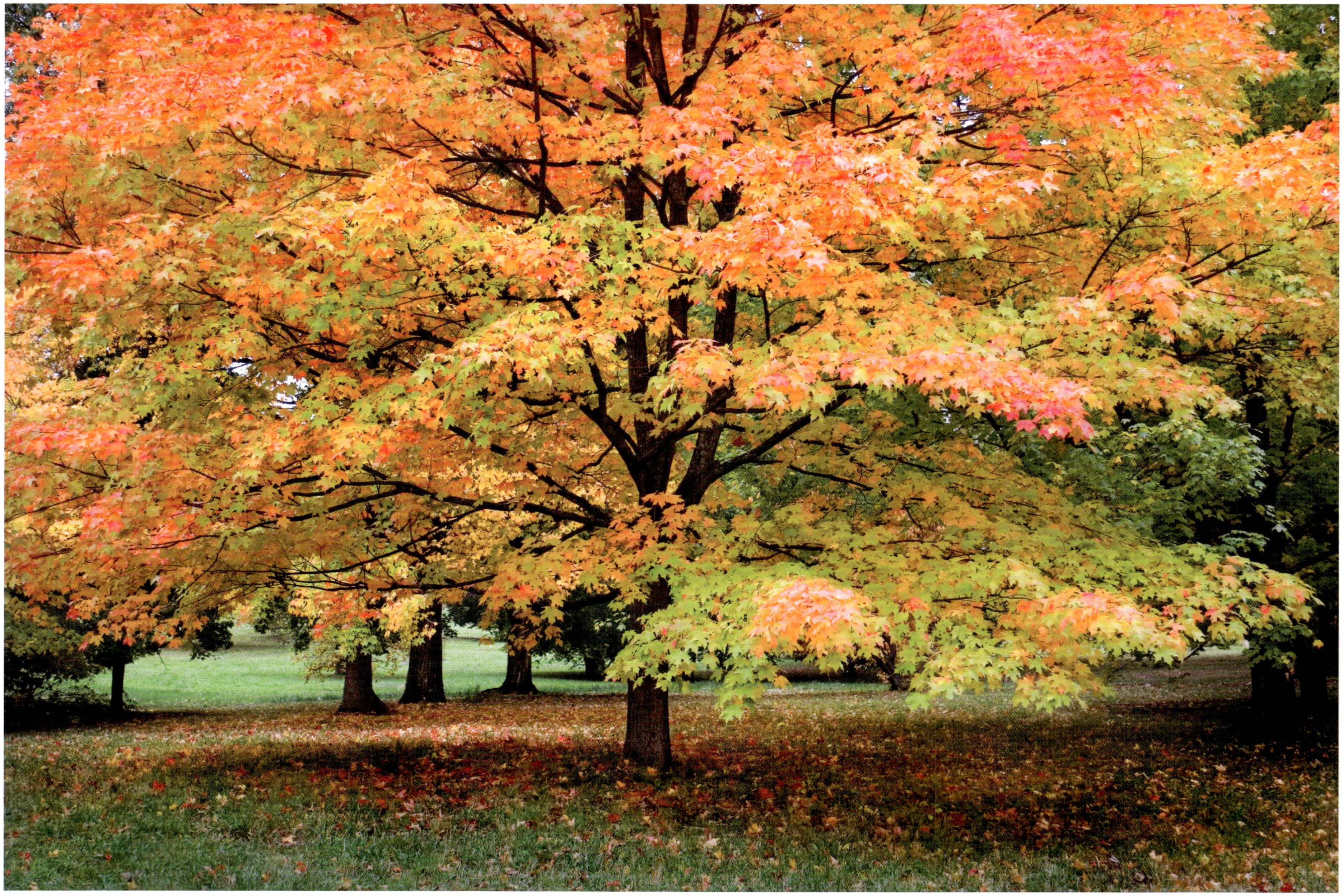

57. *First Color*, Maple Collection, 2005

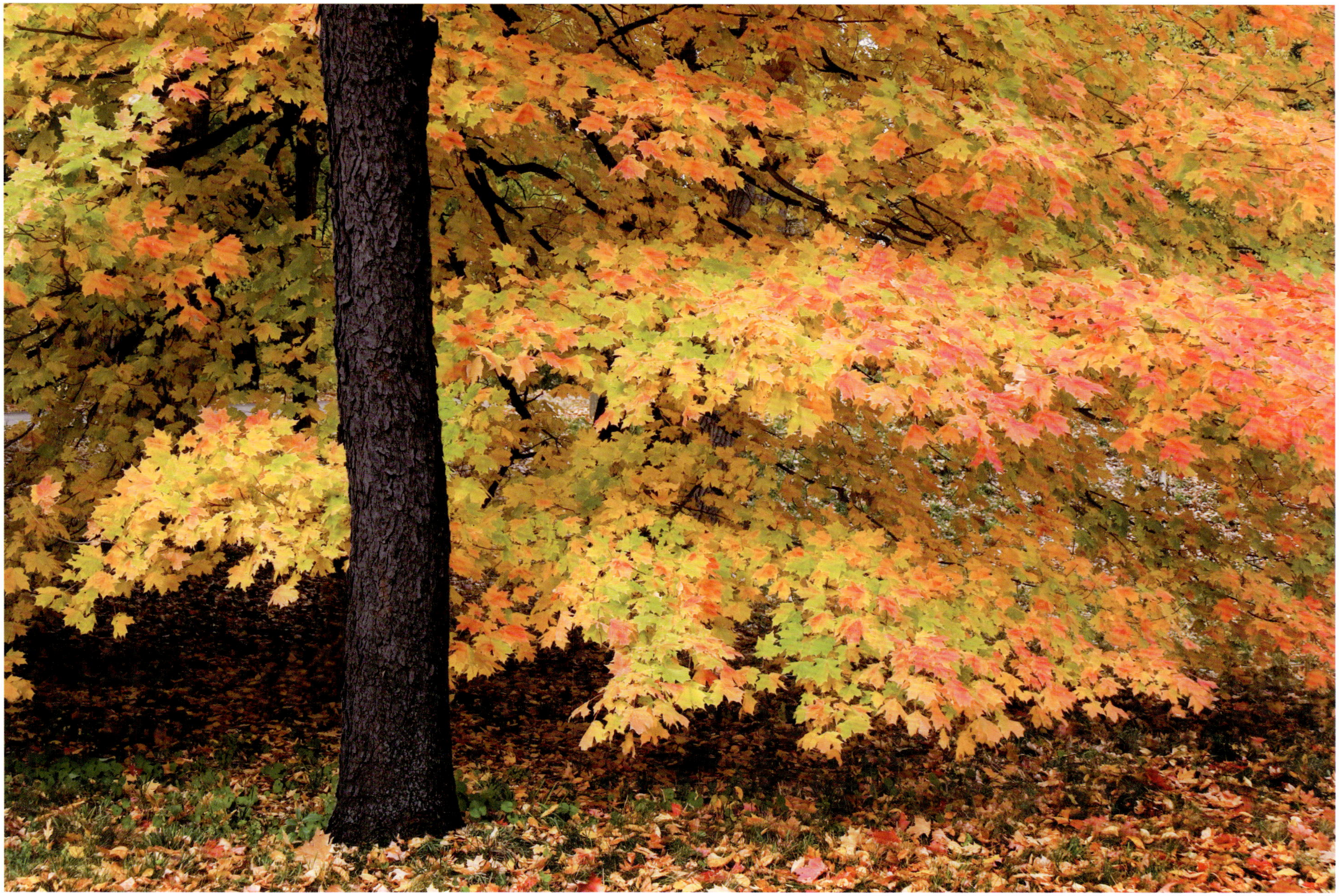

58. *Maple Branches with Hickory Trunk*, near Parking Area P31, 2005

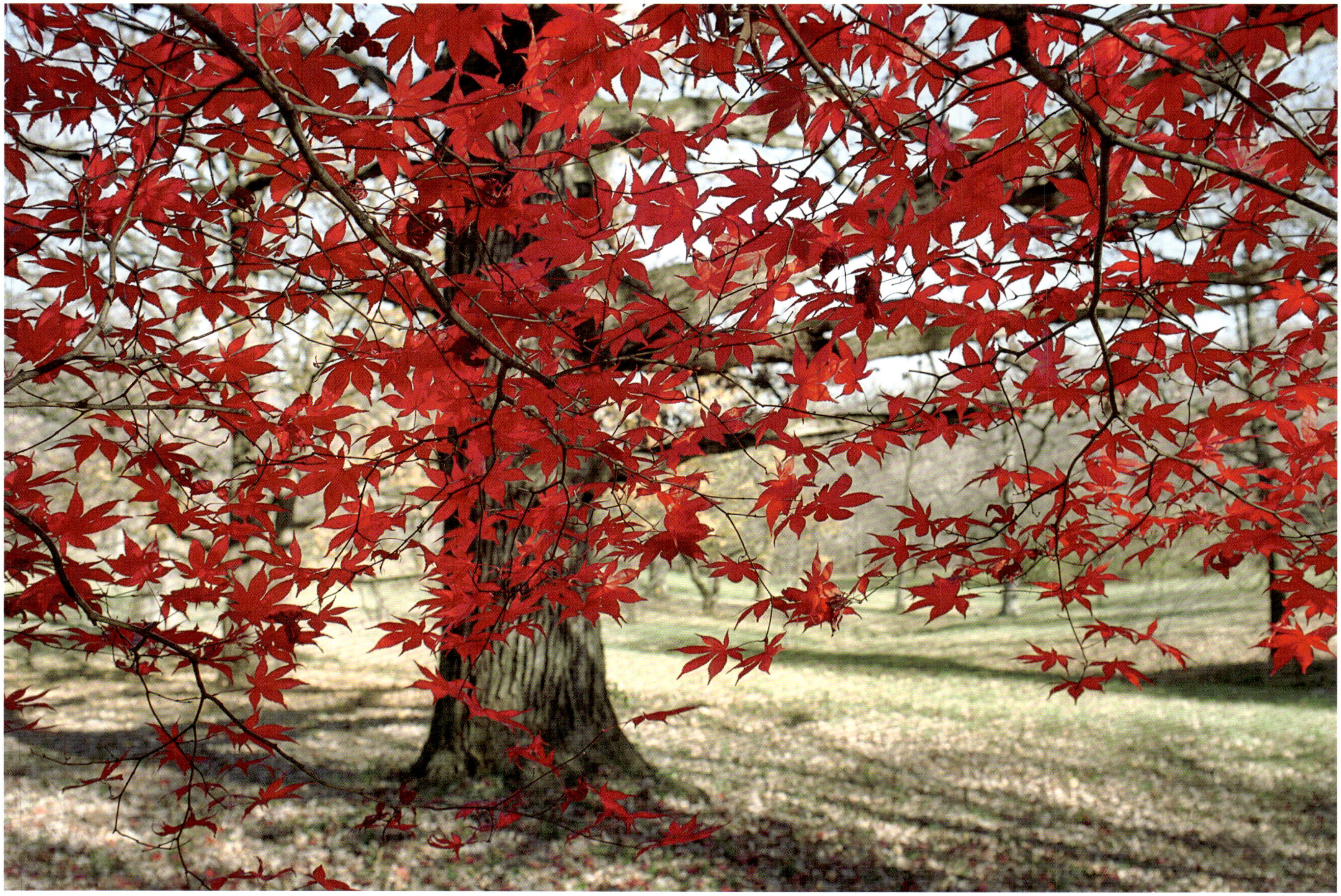

59. *Japanese Maple Branches*, Maple Glade, November 2002

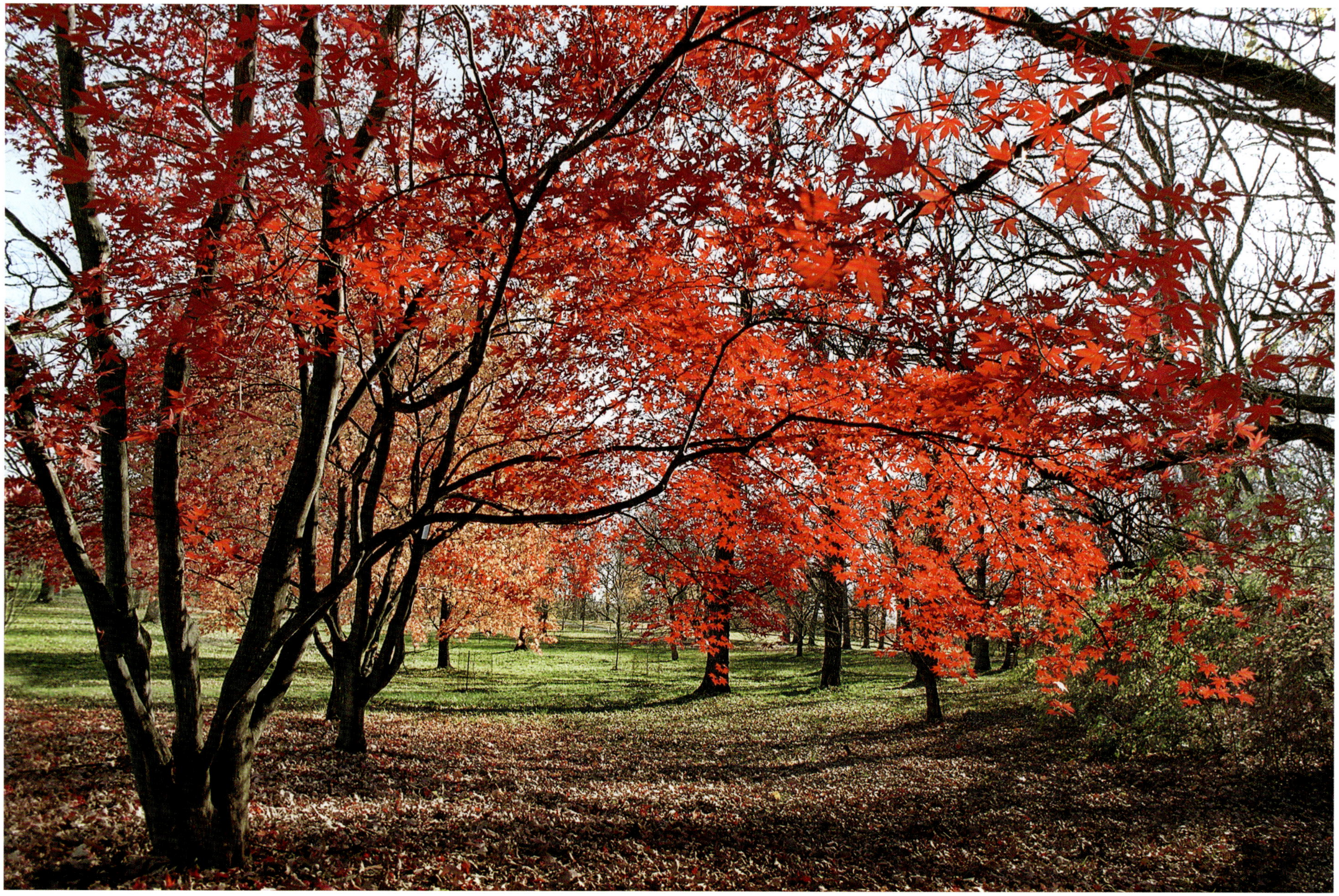

60. *Japanese Maple Trees*, November 2002

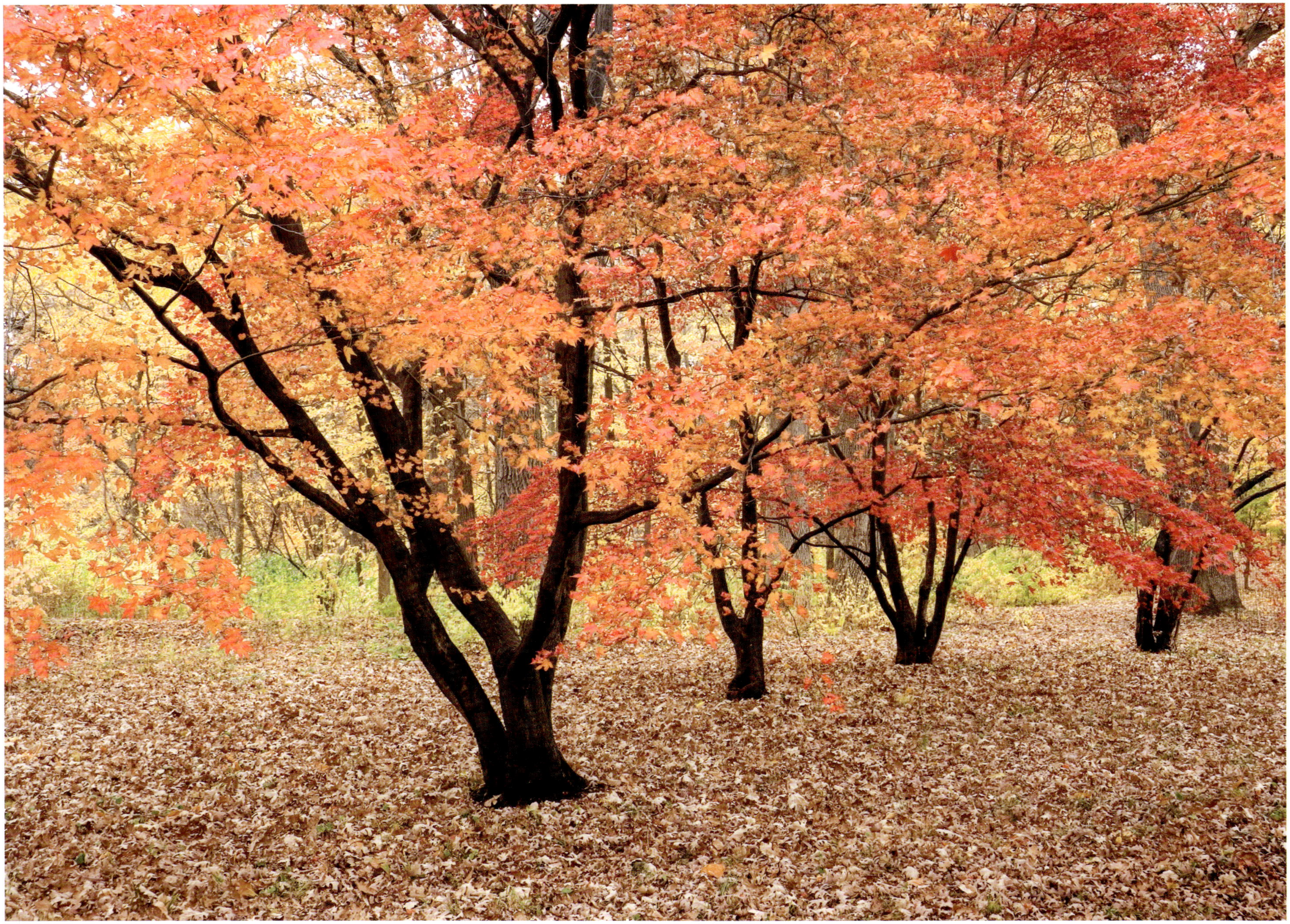

61. *Four Japanese Maples*, Maple Glade, Early November 2005

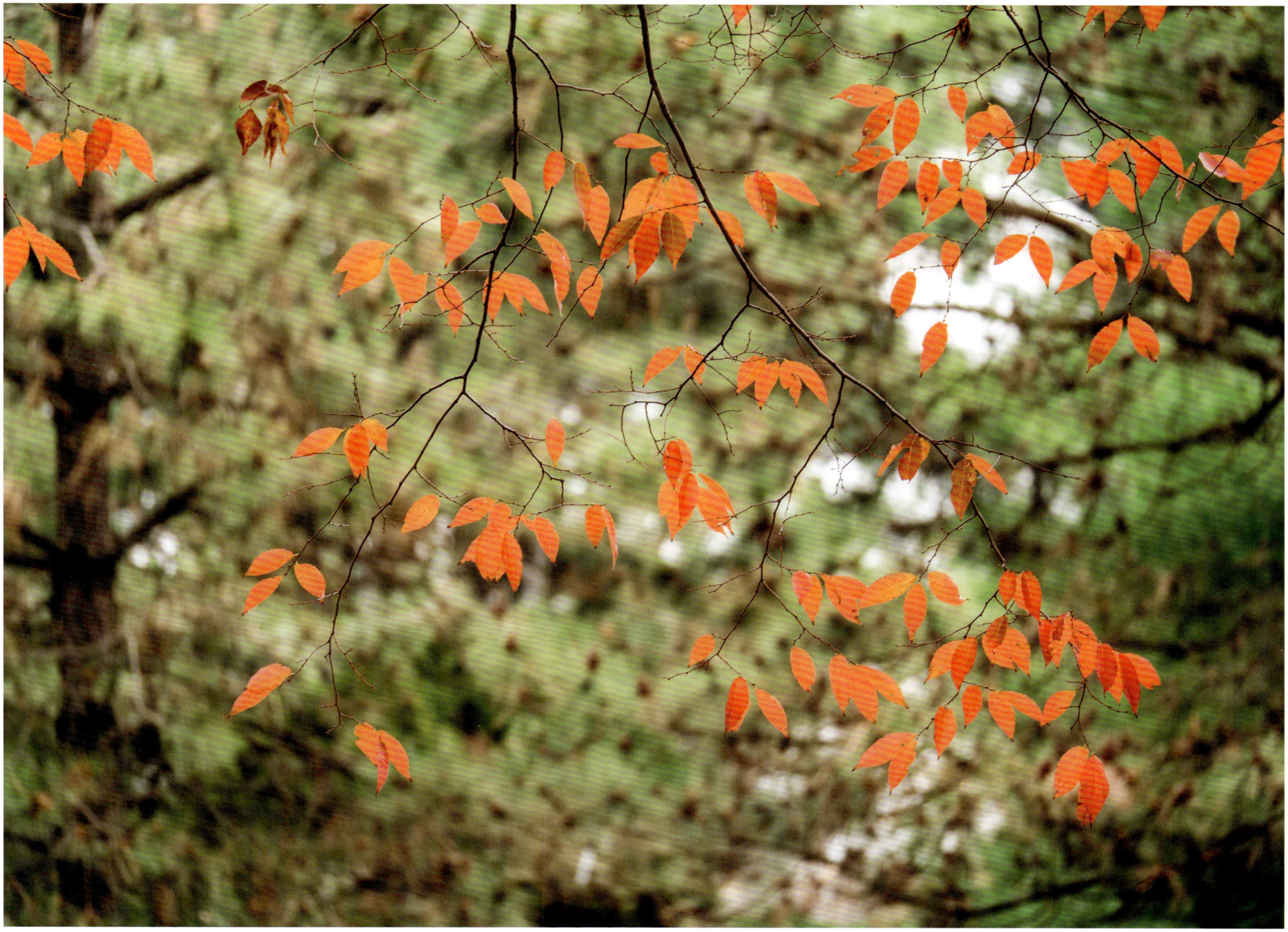

62. *Japanese Zelkova Leaves*, atop Frost Hill, 2015

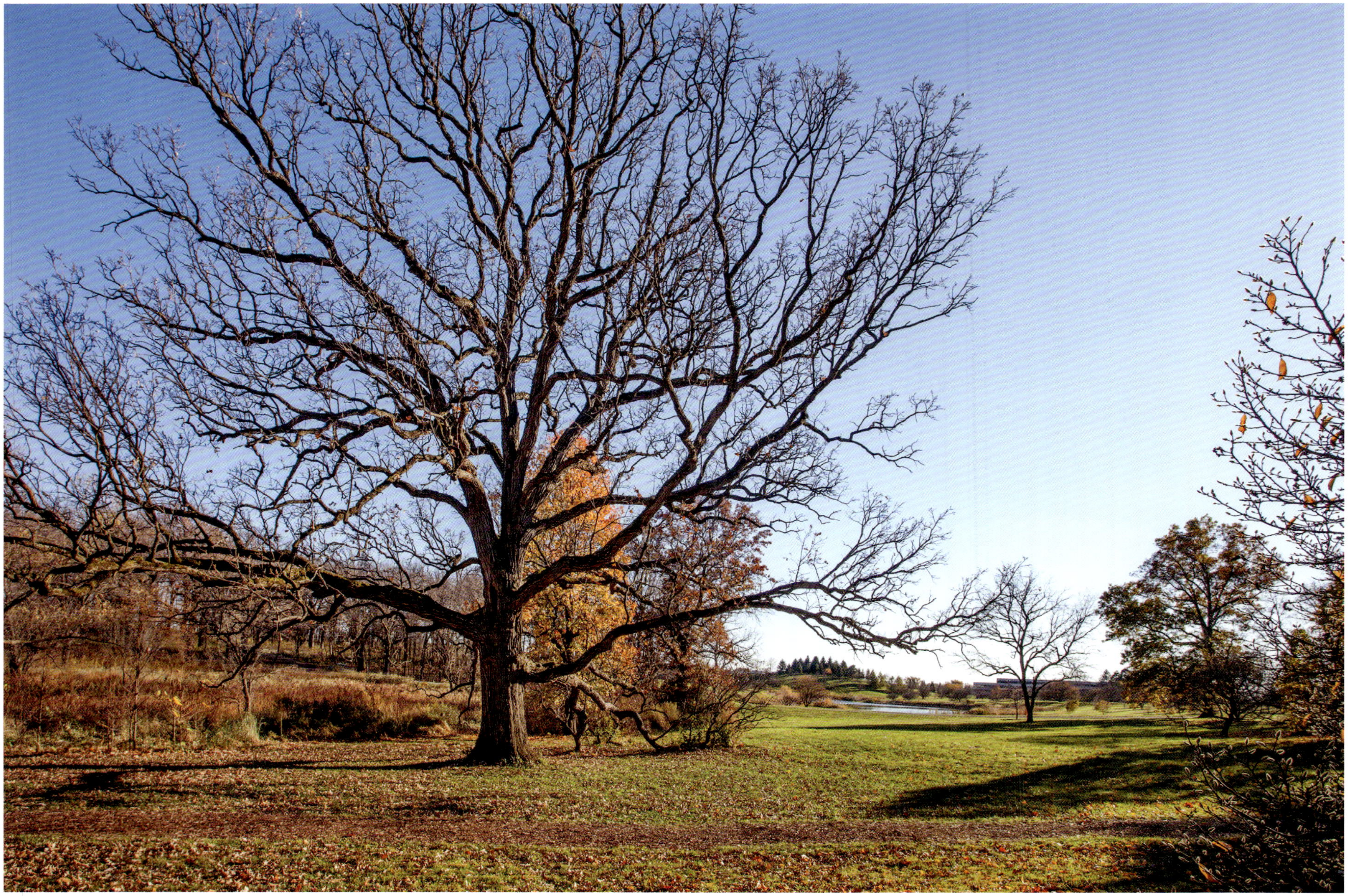

63. *Great Oak*, Late November 2014

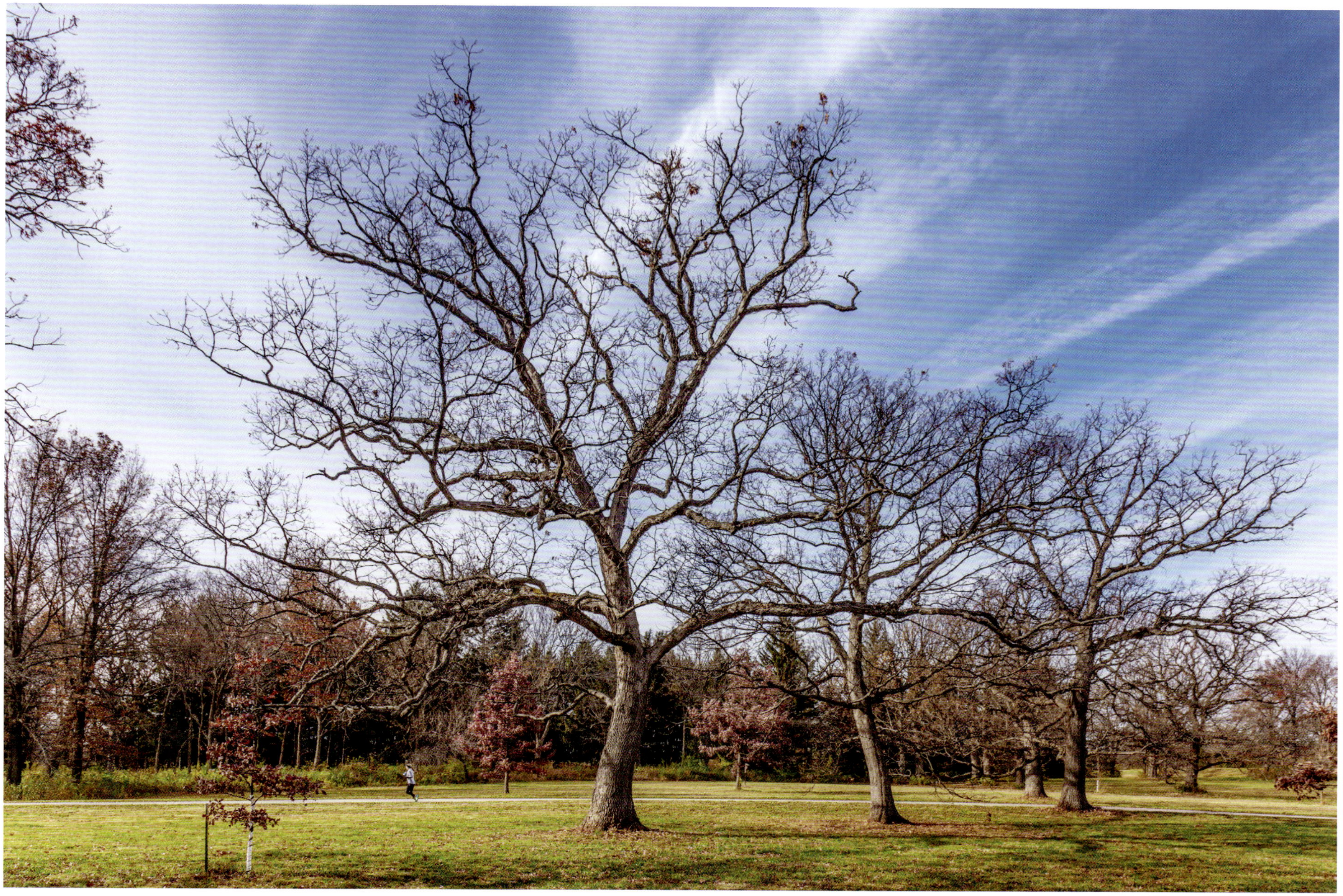

64. *Lone Runner*, December 2014

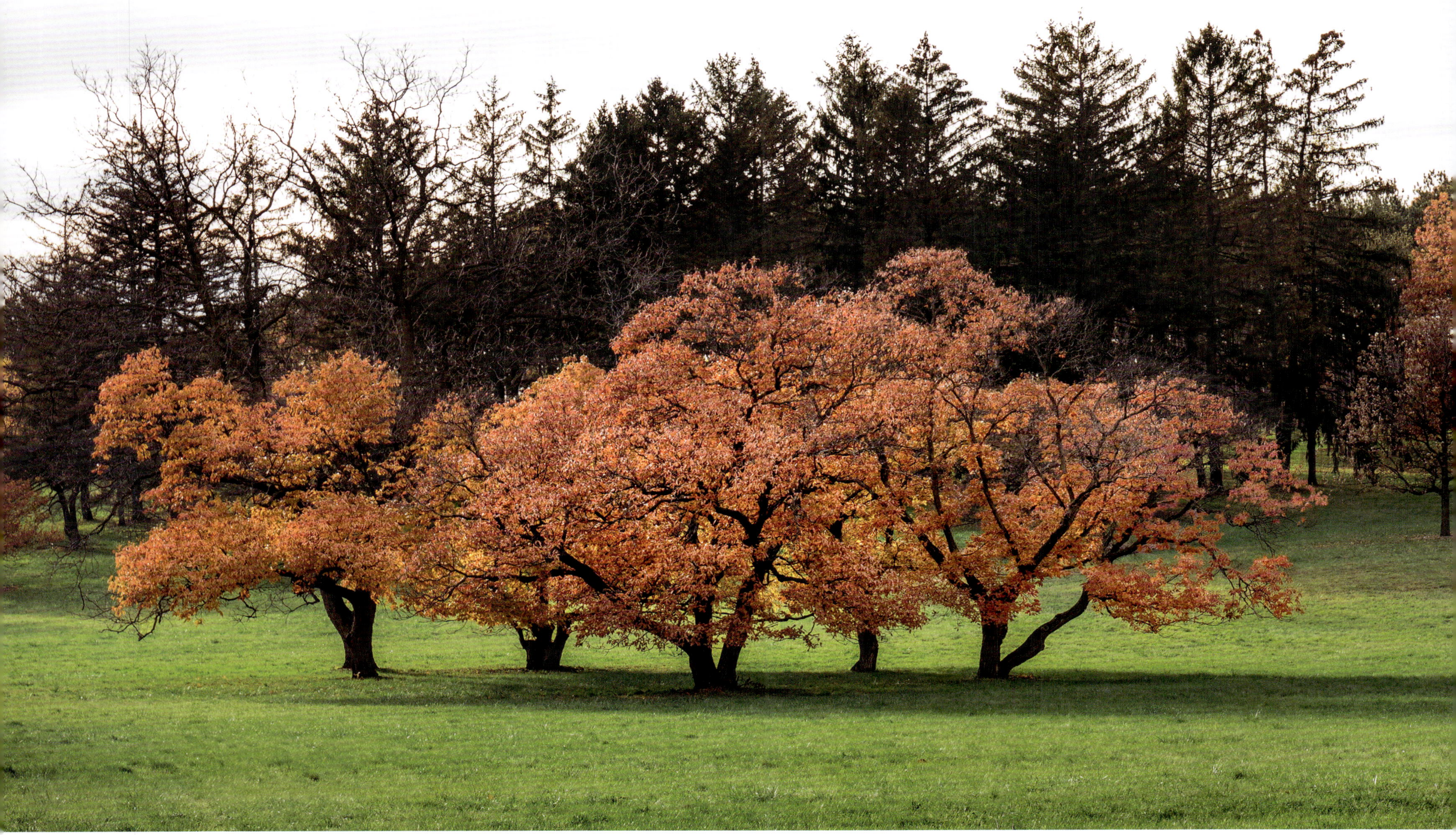

65. *Five Chestnut Trees, Bobolink Meadow, November 2017*

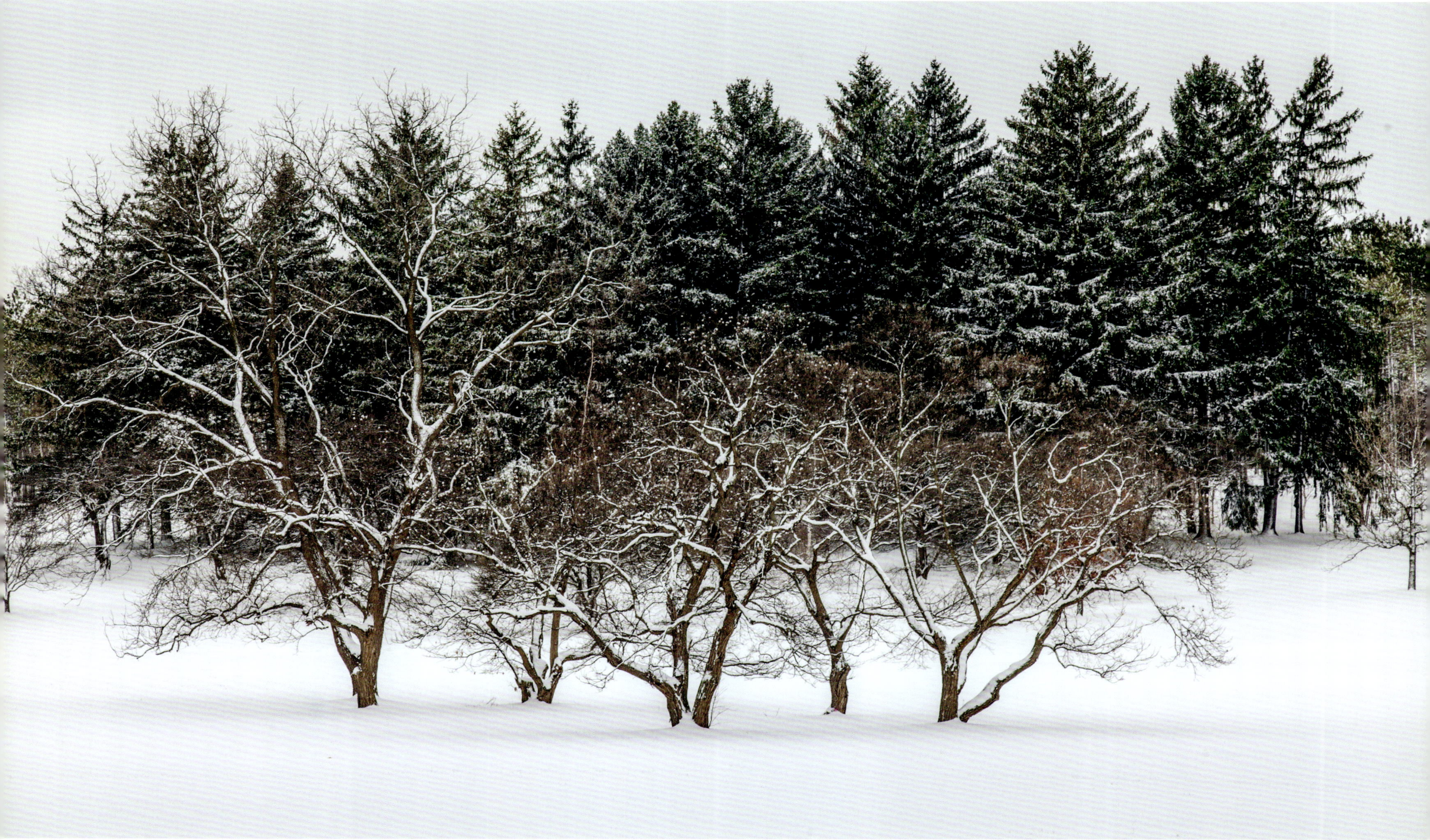

66. *Five Chestnut Trees, Bobolink Meadow, January 2015*

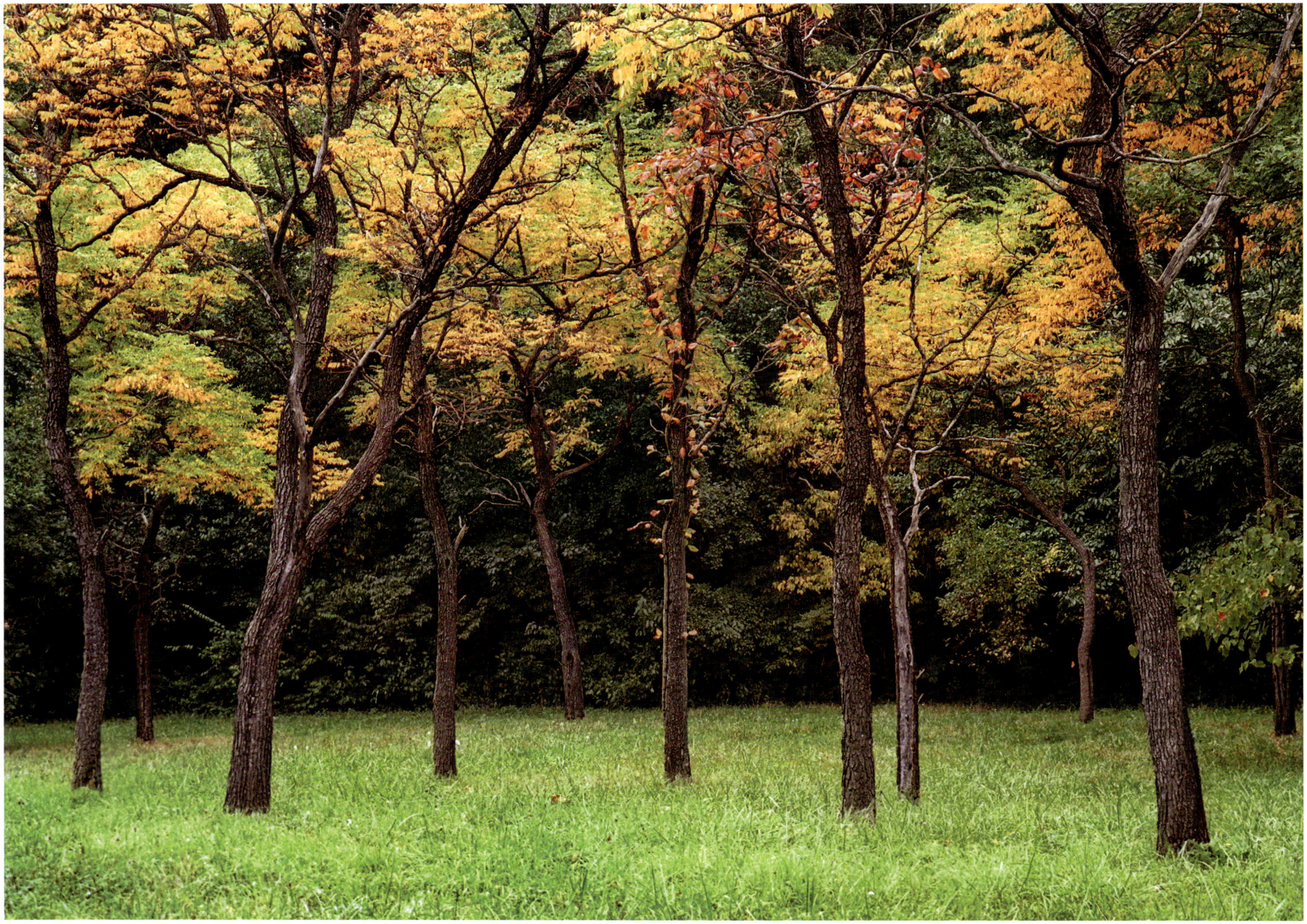

67. *Eleven Trees*, East Side, 2007

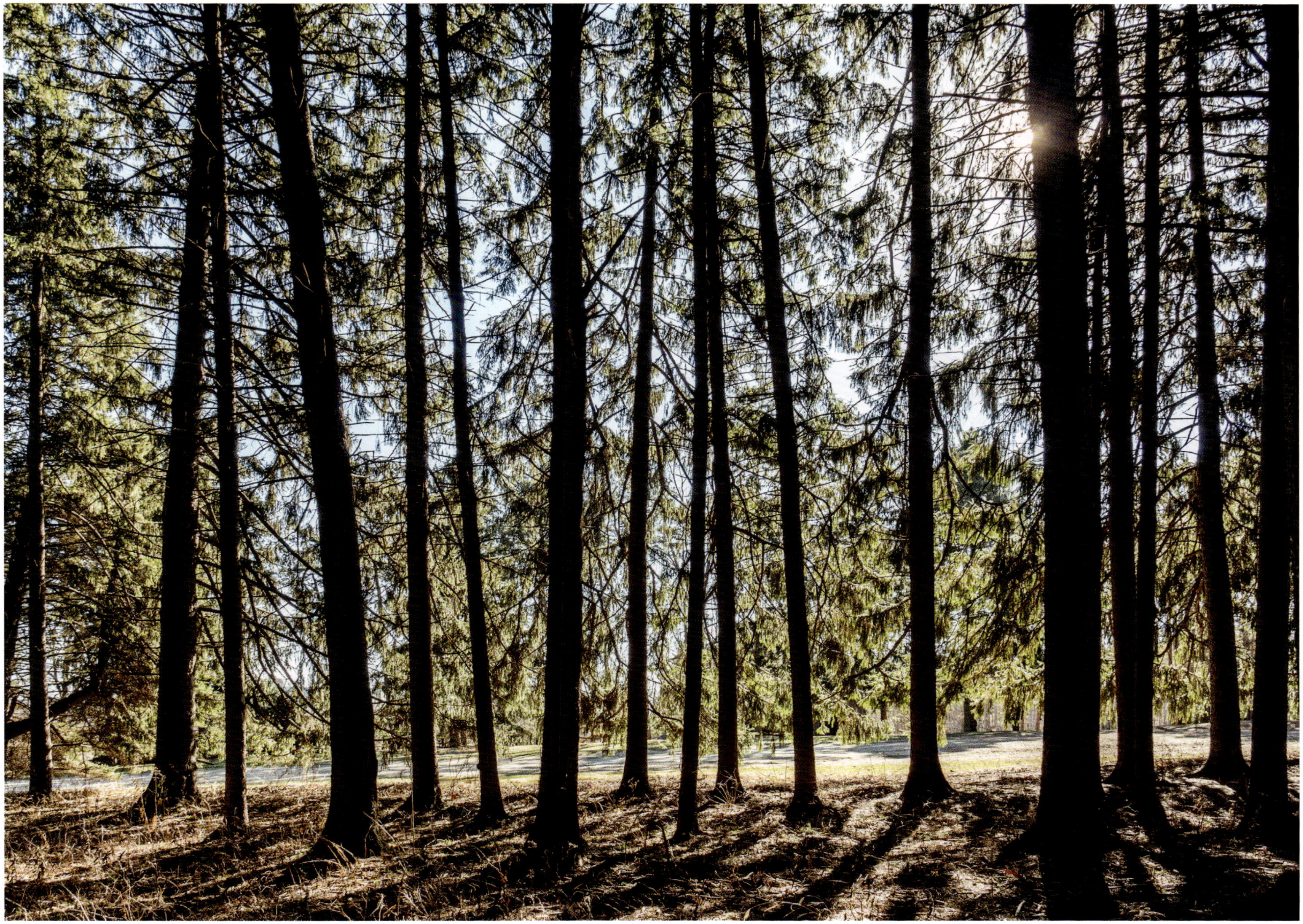

68. *Spruce Stand*, at Parking Area P29, 2017

9

THE STORY OF A WINTER PICTURE

Falling snow makes visual magic happen.

Excited by a late-winter snow forecast the night before, I grabbed my camera the next morning and headed for the Arboretum. As large, heavy snowflakes hit my windshield, I started to picture my favorite places with snow falling on them and wondered which one to choose. I couldn't wait to see the particular magic that today's falling snow would create on my last chance for a winter picture that year, April 9, 2018.

In case the day's treasure (falling snow) turned out to be short-lived, I decided on the location I could get to fastest: the path around Meadow Lake. As I jumped out of my car, wet snowflakes chilled my face, and snow-filled air deadened the sound of mid-morning traffic. With every step, I enjoyed seeing lightly frosted individual branches nearby and, in the distance, dark evergreens now impressionistically softened and brightened by falling snow. About half way around the lake, something stopped me. I looked back and saw a V-shaped tree (Plate 69) that I had never noticed before on my many trips around the lake. Why did I notice it this time? I wasn't thinking symmetry; I was thinking snow. Perhaps it stood out because snow-filled air was making all those distant evergreens behind it so much lighter and less distinct?

I was intrigued and walked back to look closer. I changed to a wide-angle lens so I could stay close and still include most of the tree in a wide view of the lake. I moved back and forth a bit, watching the screen. Then I looked beyond the tree, taking a moment to breathe and watch the snow falling through the air over the lake. Then, rechecking the screen, I felt balance and completeness and pressed the shutter.

Later that day, warm and back at home, I recognized the worthiness of the V-shaped tree on my computer screen. Now I could see how together all the lines, shapes, and muted colors in the picture somehow created balance out of chaos. Since then, whenever I look at the picture, I see more reasons why I love it. Symmetry is not a goal, but it is a visual friend. The picture is loaded with reflection-created symmetries, repeating V-shapes, and two evergreen branches that seem to wave at each other from one corner of the picture to another.

And then there is the perched robin. Though I only consciously noticed her much later, I'm sure that her presence was part of the balance and completeness I felt when I pressed the shutter.

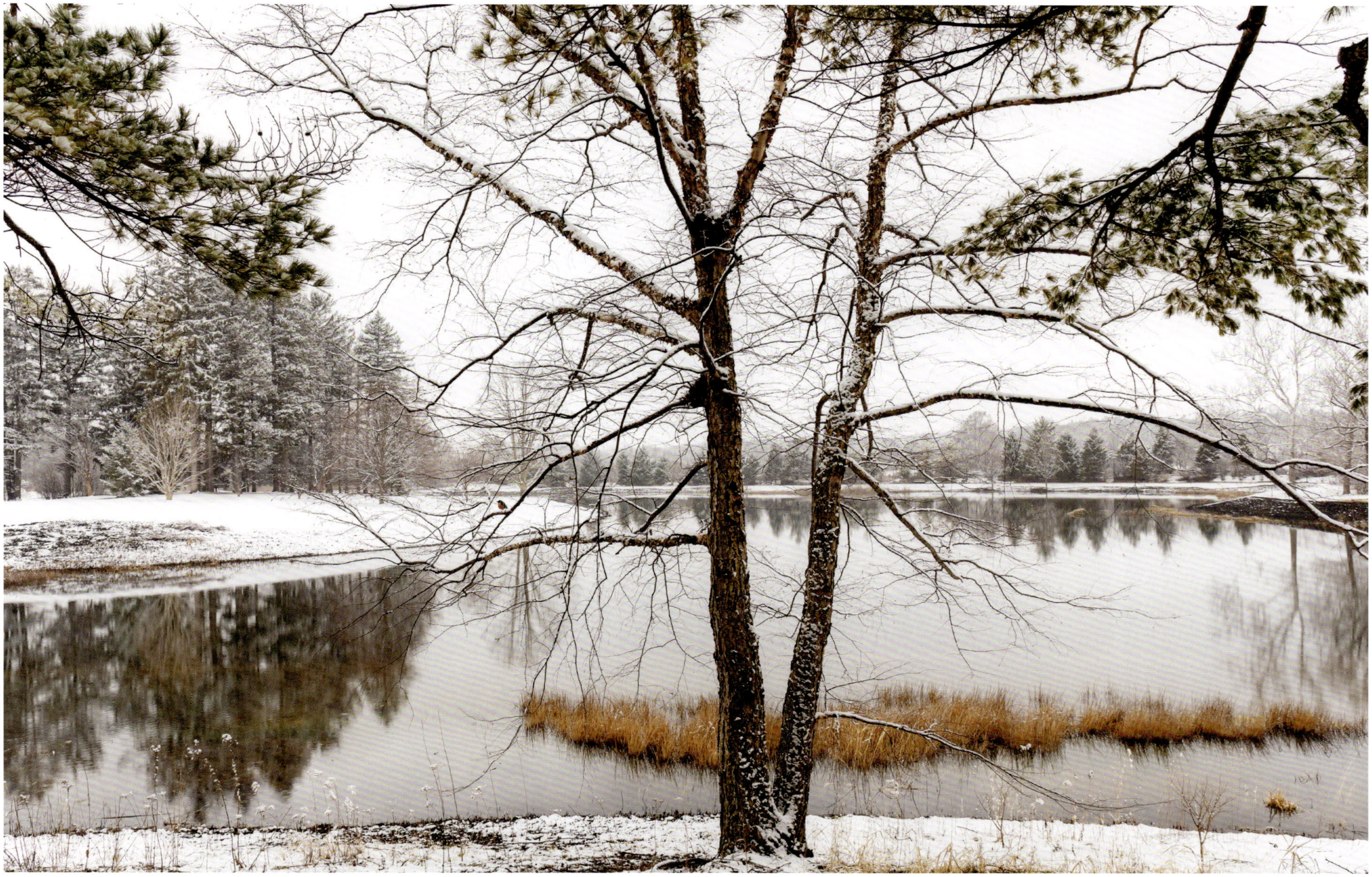

69. *April Snow on Meadow Lake*, 2018

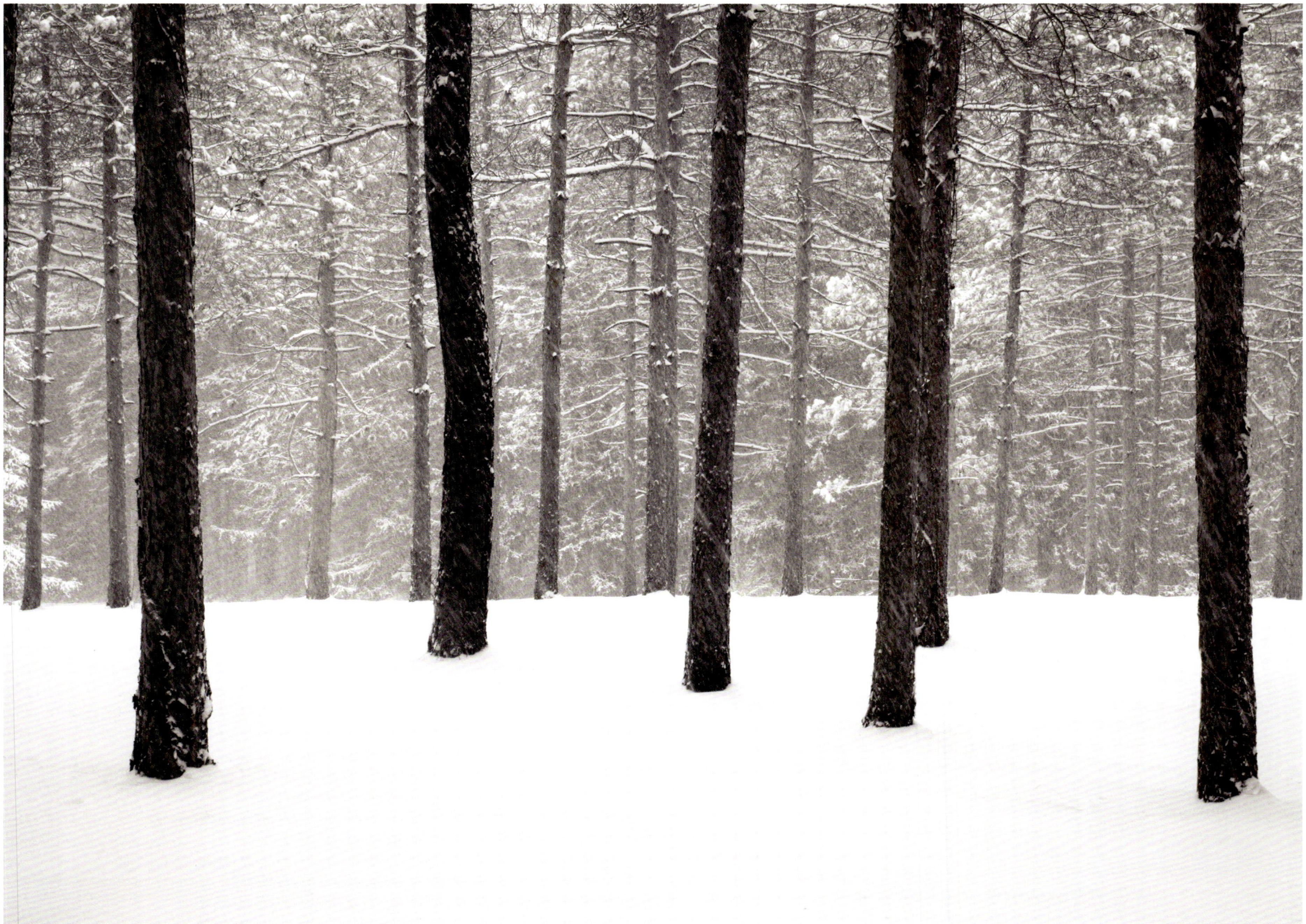

70. *Snow Fall on Spruce Hill*, near Parking Area P29, 2017

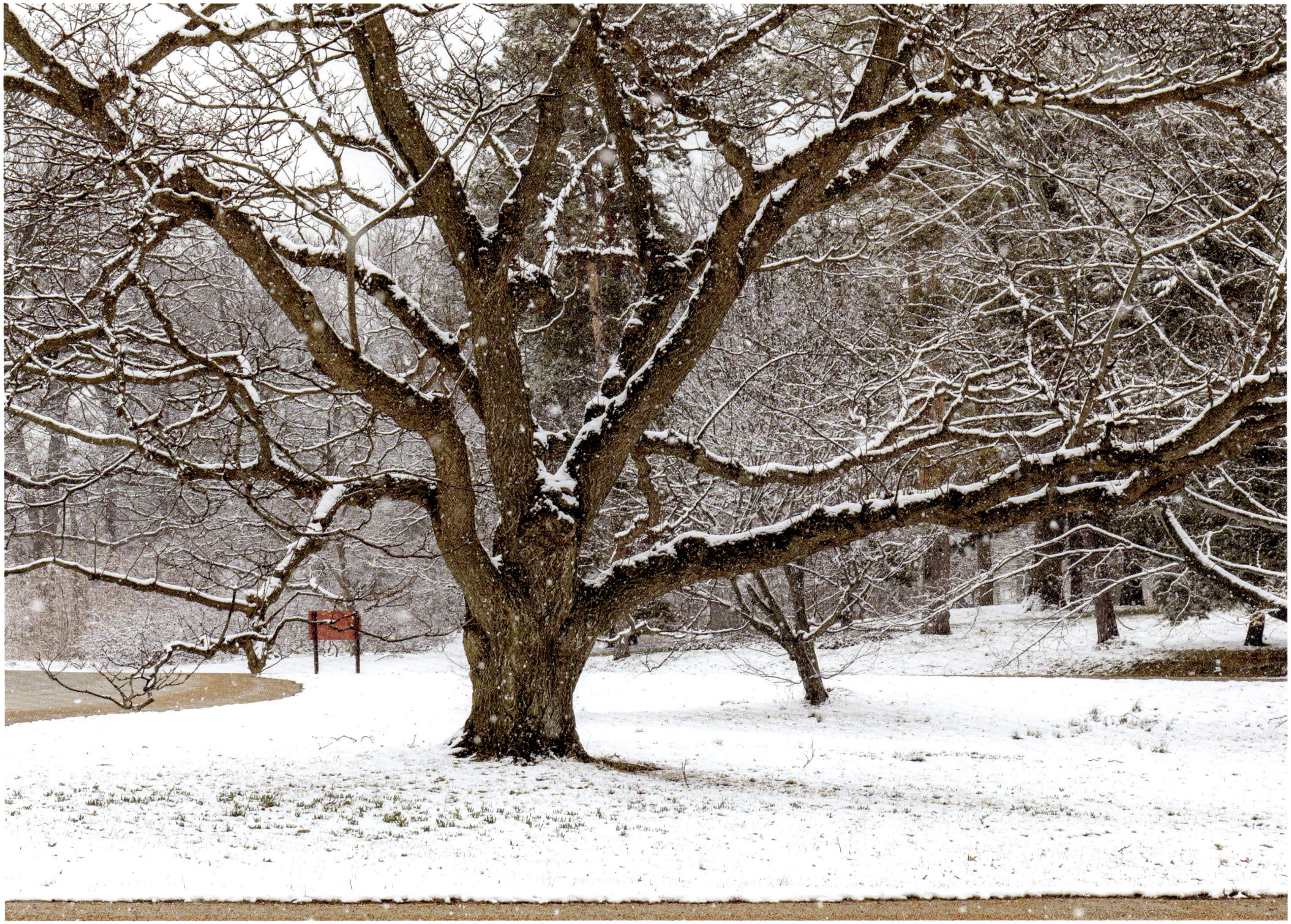

71. *Cork Tree and Snowflakes at the Intersection*, East Side, 2018

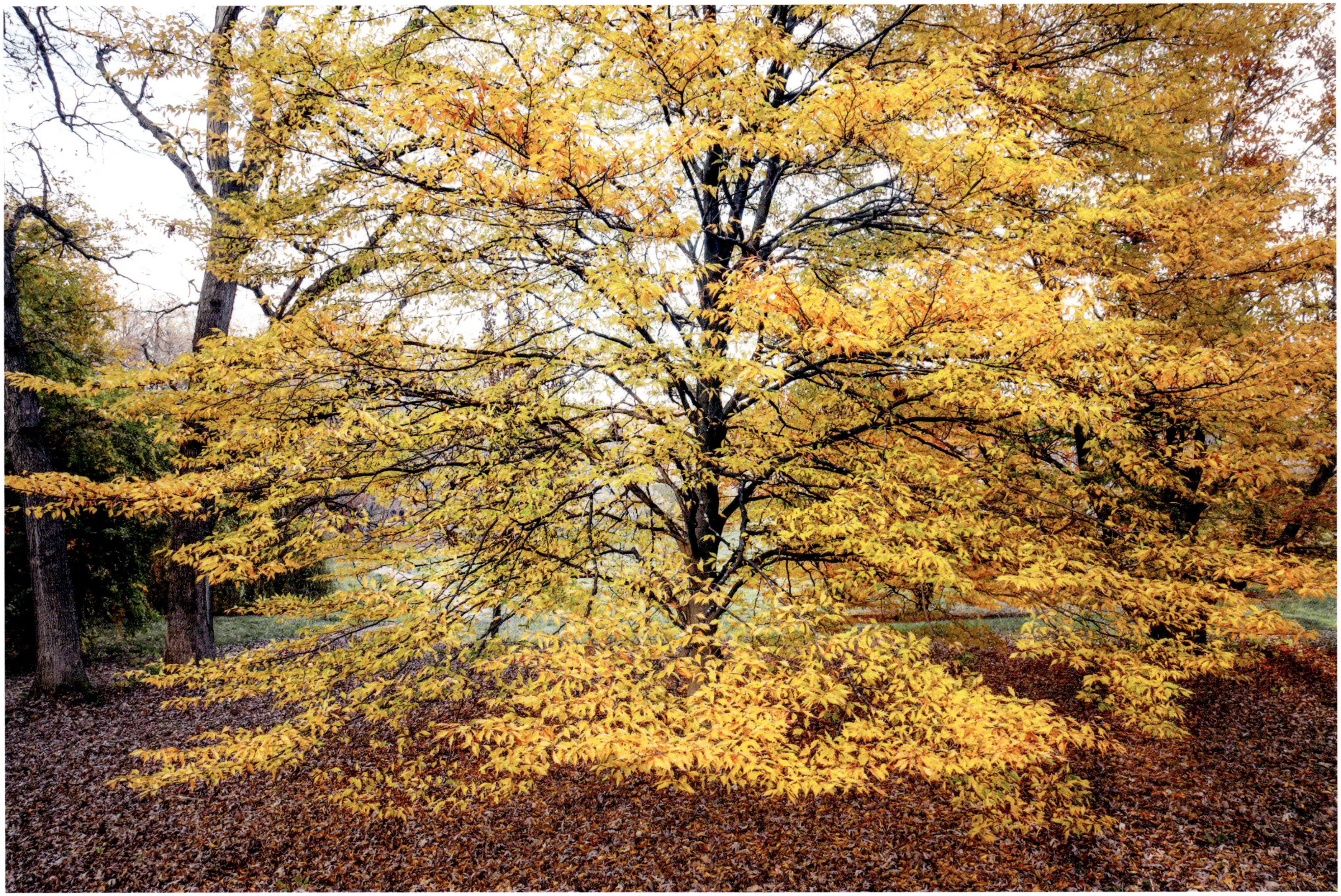

72. *Cut-Leaf European Beech*, Late October 2012

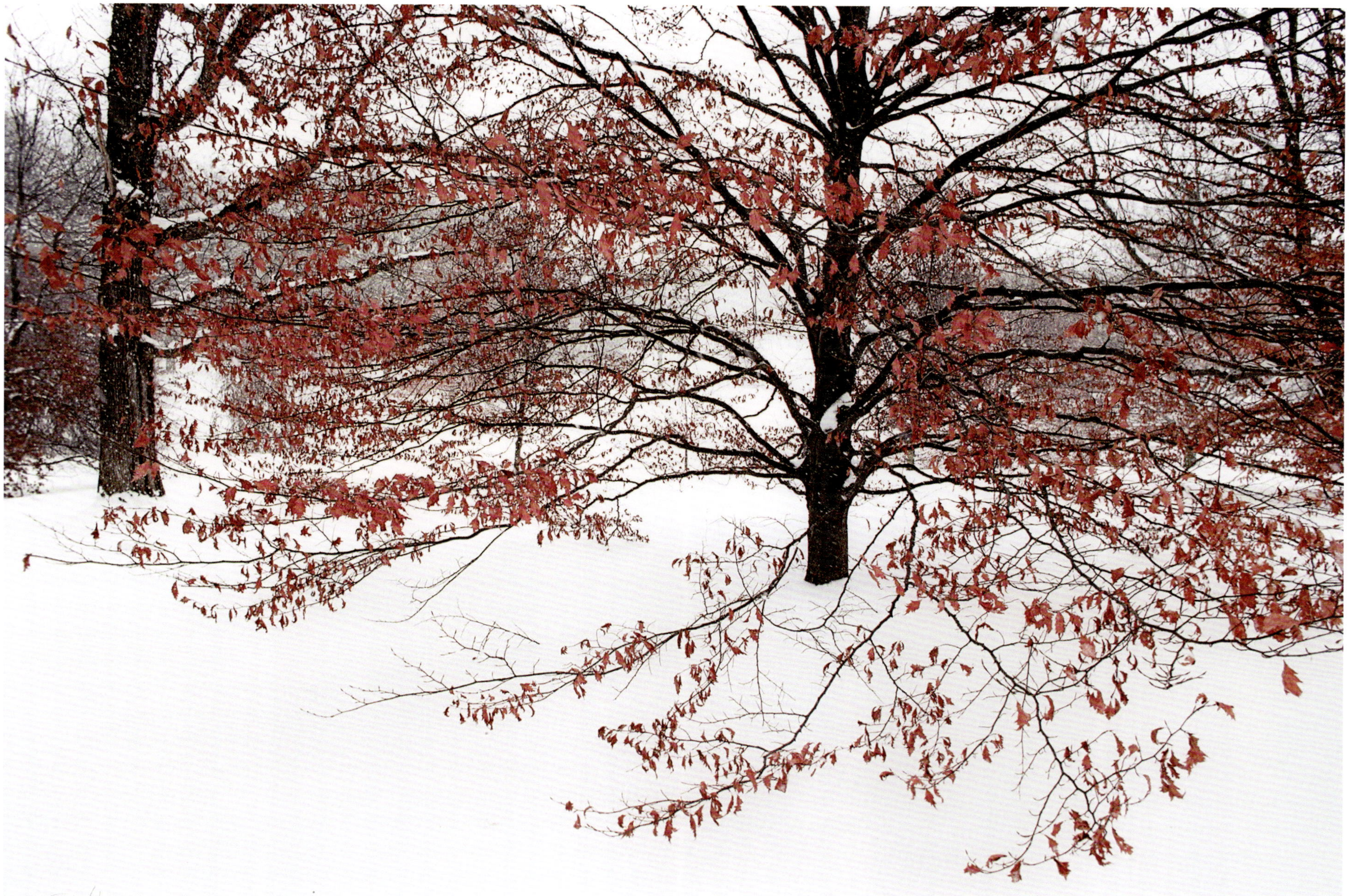

73. *Cut-Leaf European Beech in December Snowfall*, 2001

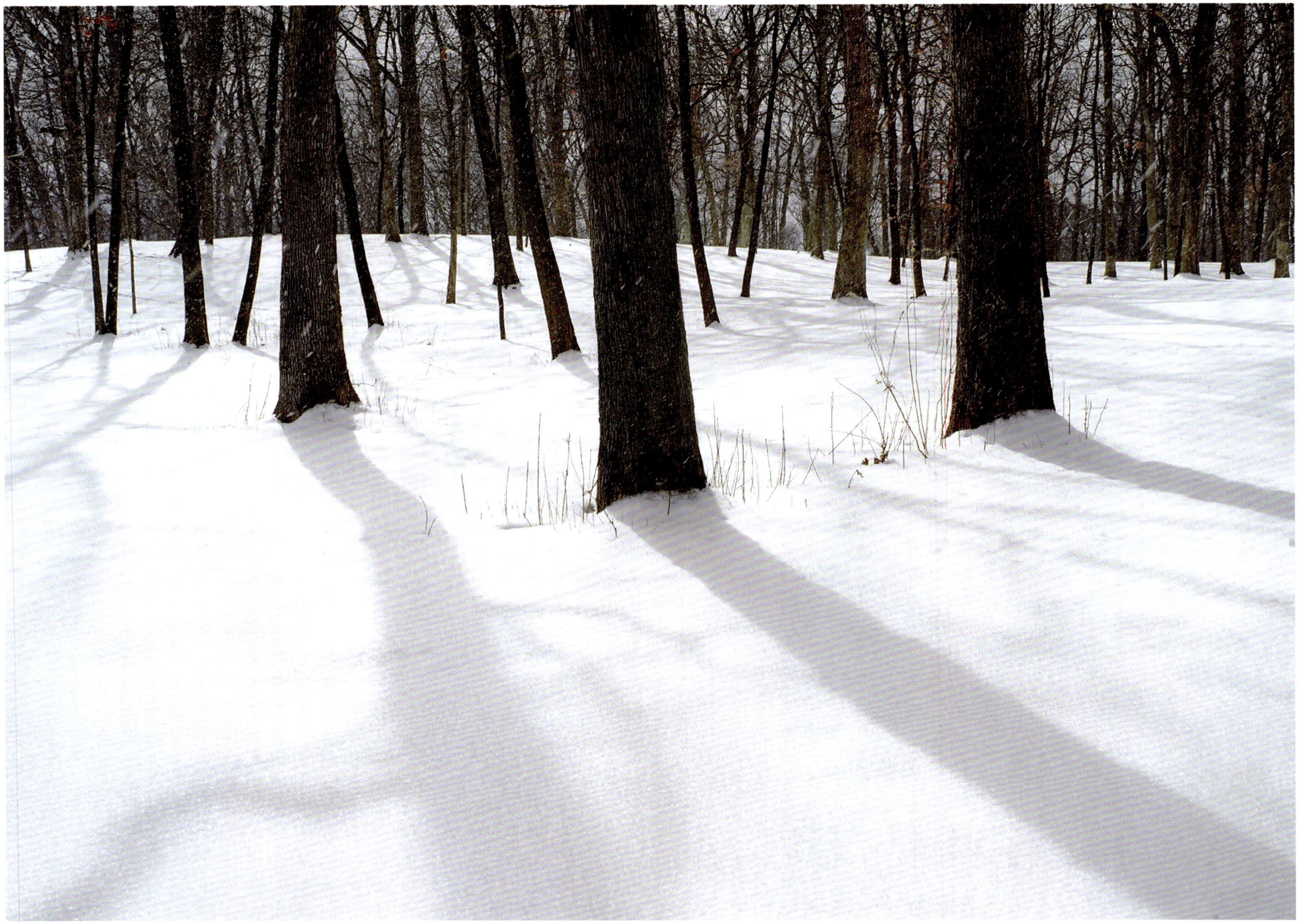

74. *Snow in the Air, Shadows on the Snow*, 2004

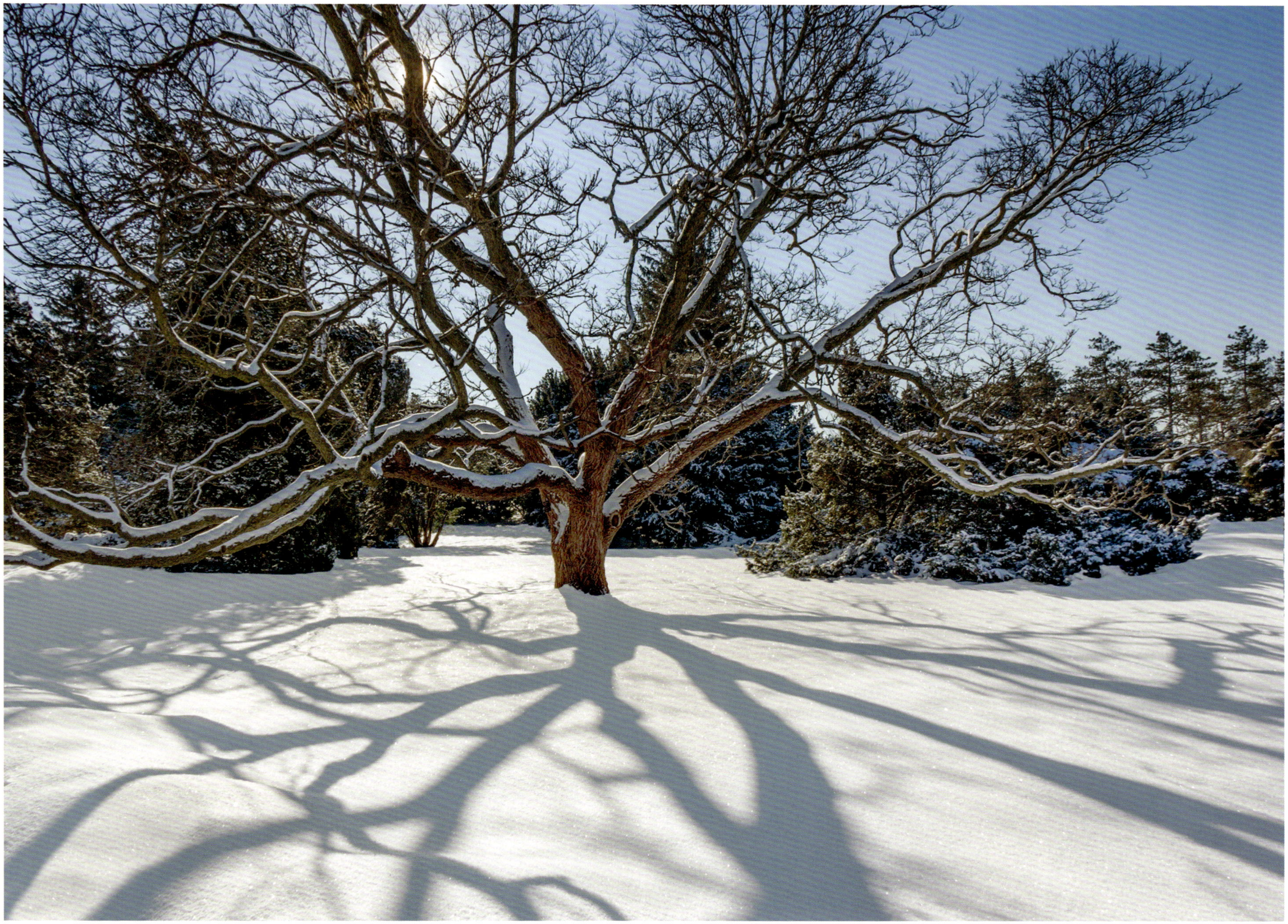

75. *Cork Tree in New Snow*, near the Hedge Collection, 2008

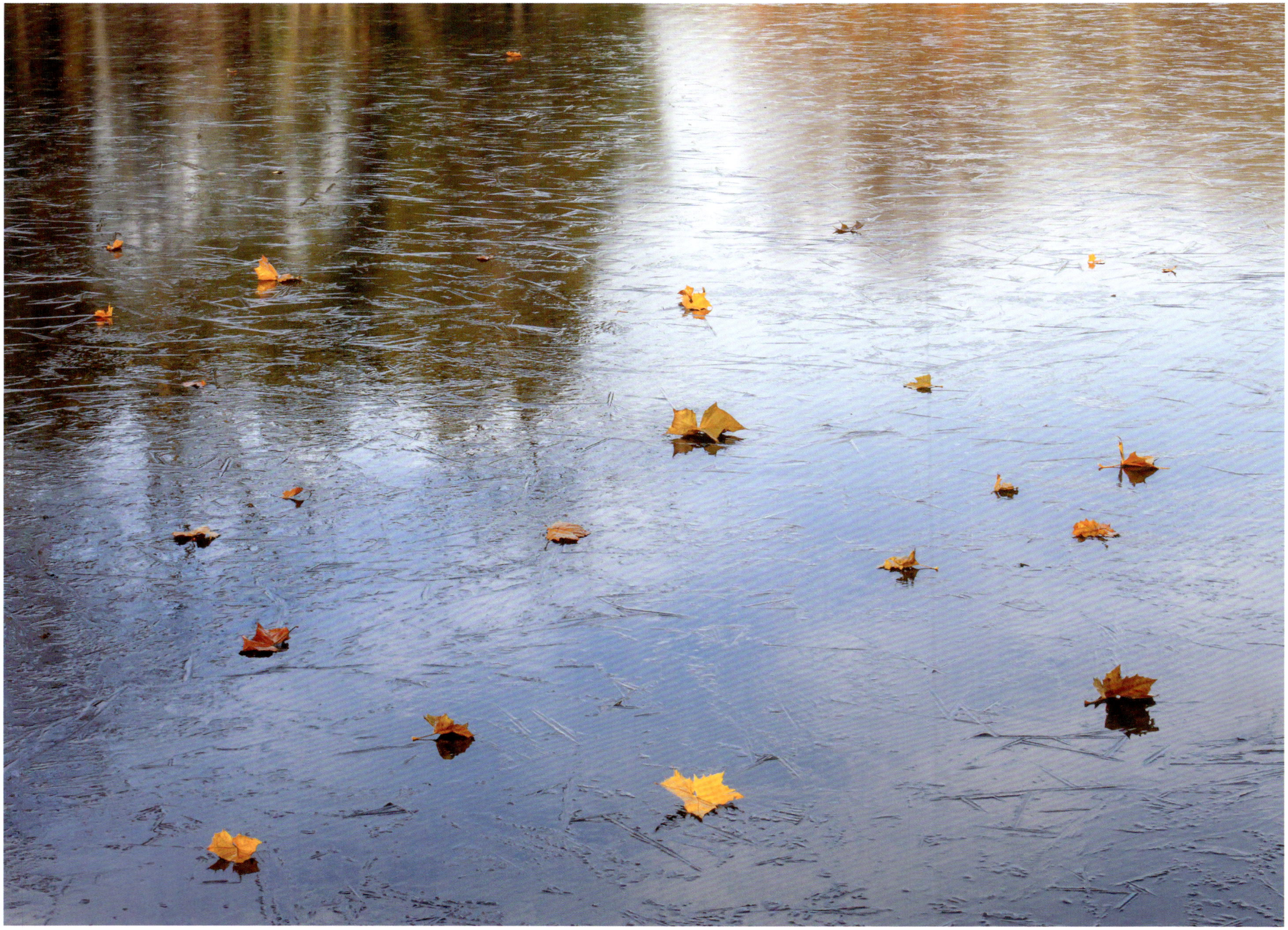

76. *Leaves on Frozen Lake Marmo*, 2017

77. *Floating Leaves*, below Bridge at Rainbow Falls, 2012 (opposite)

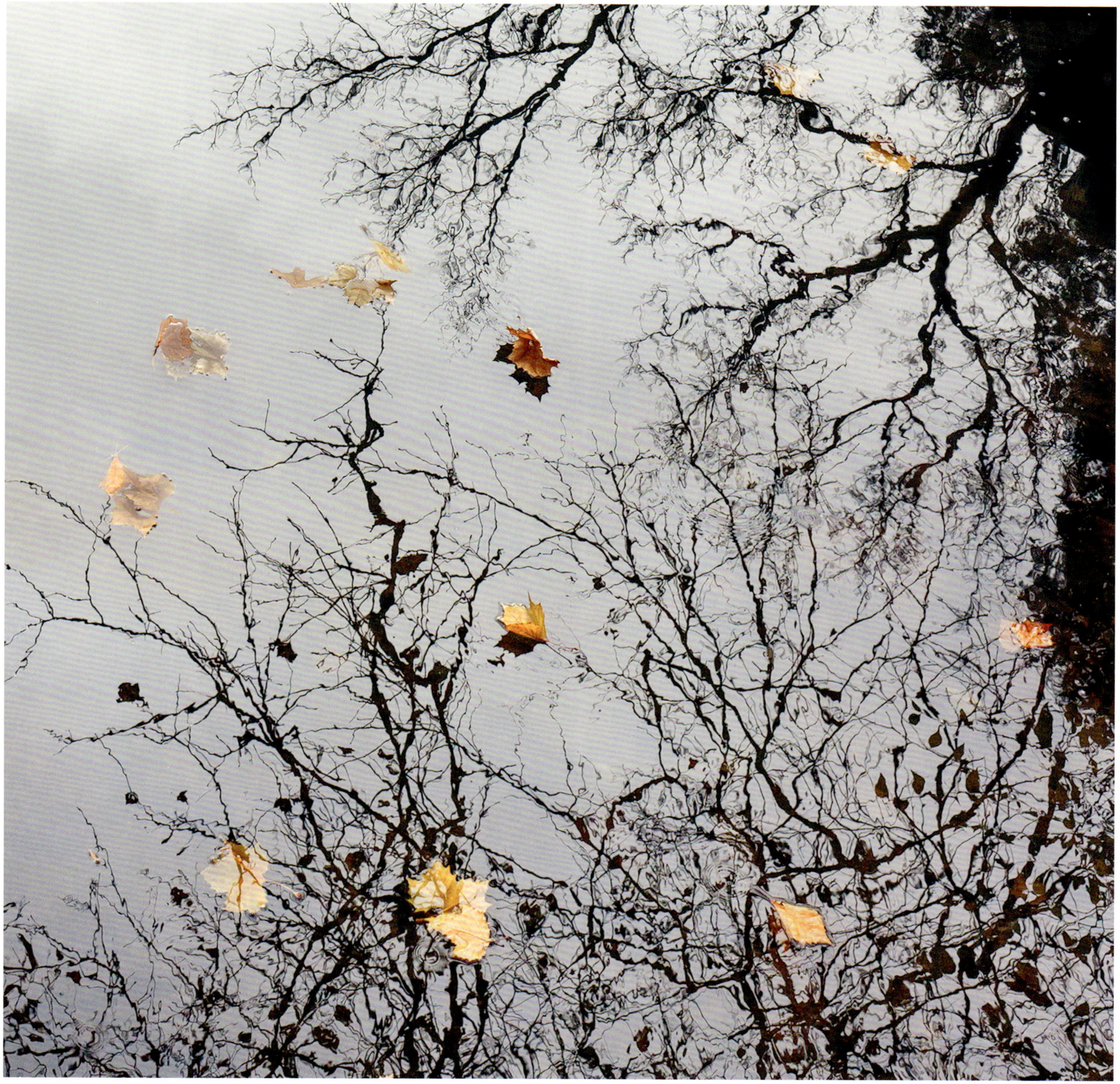

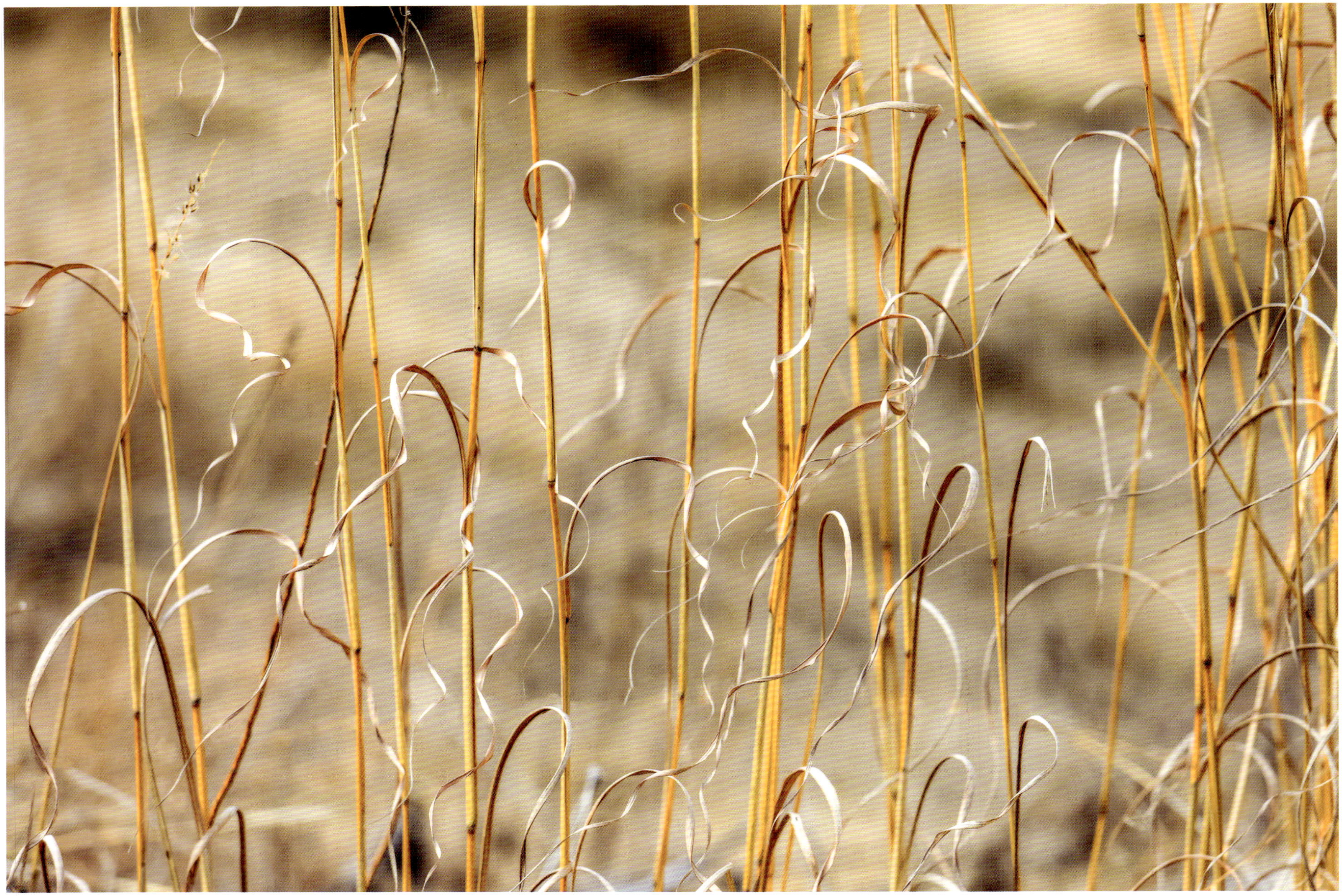

78. *Spent Grass*, Schulenberg Prairie, 2018
79. *Willoway Flourish*, 2019 (opposite)

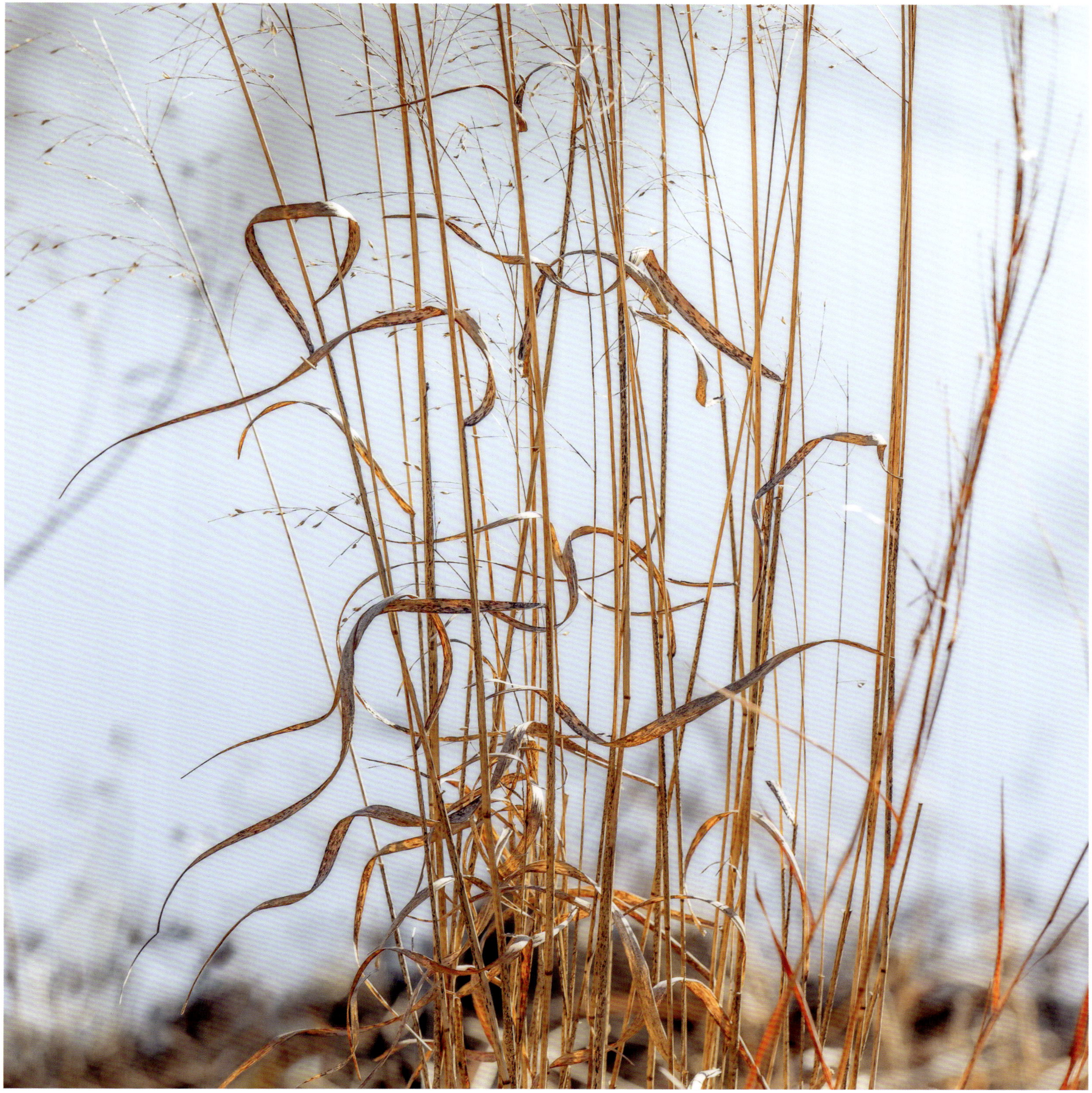

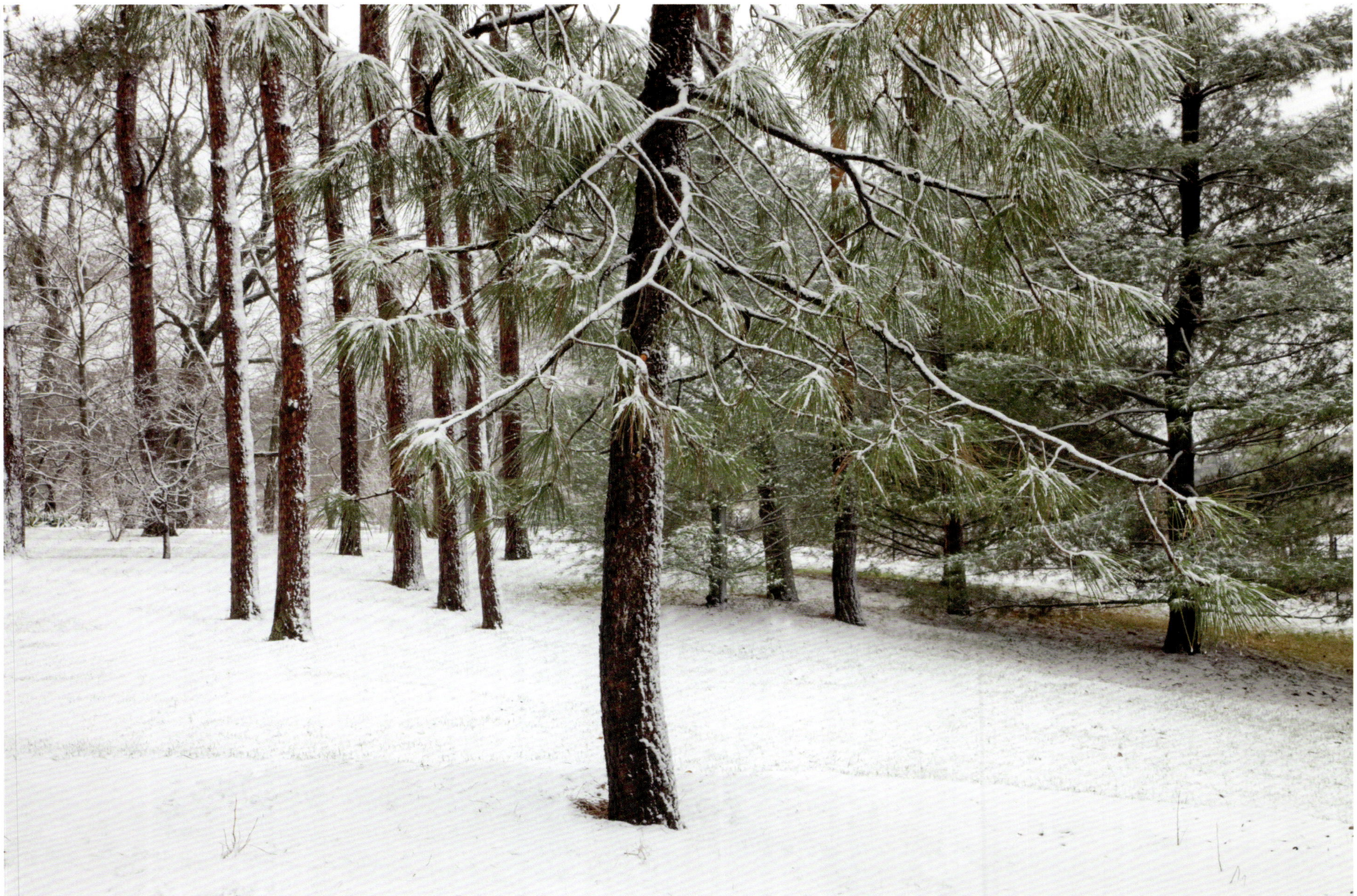

80. *Bent Pine*, near the Eastside Trailhead, 2009
81. *Pines atop Frost Hill*, East Side, 2013 (opposite)

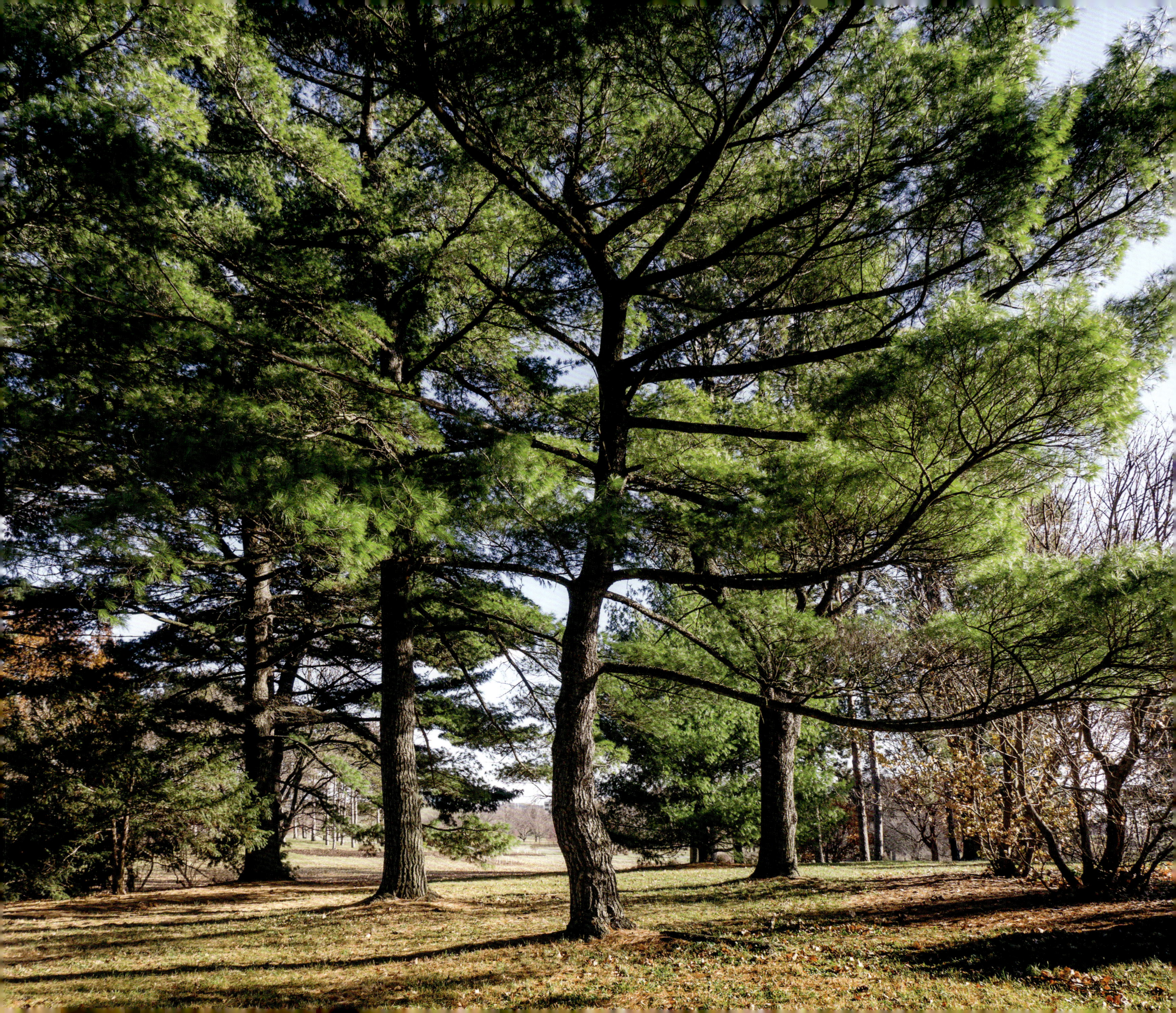

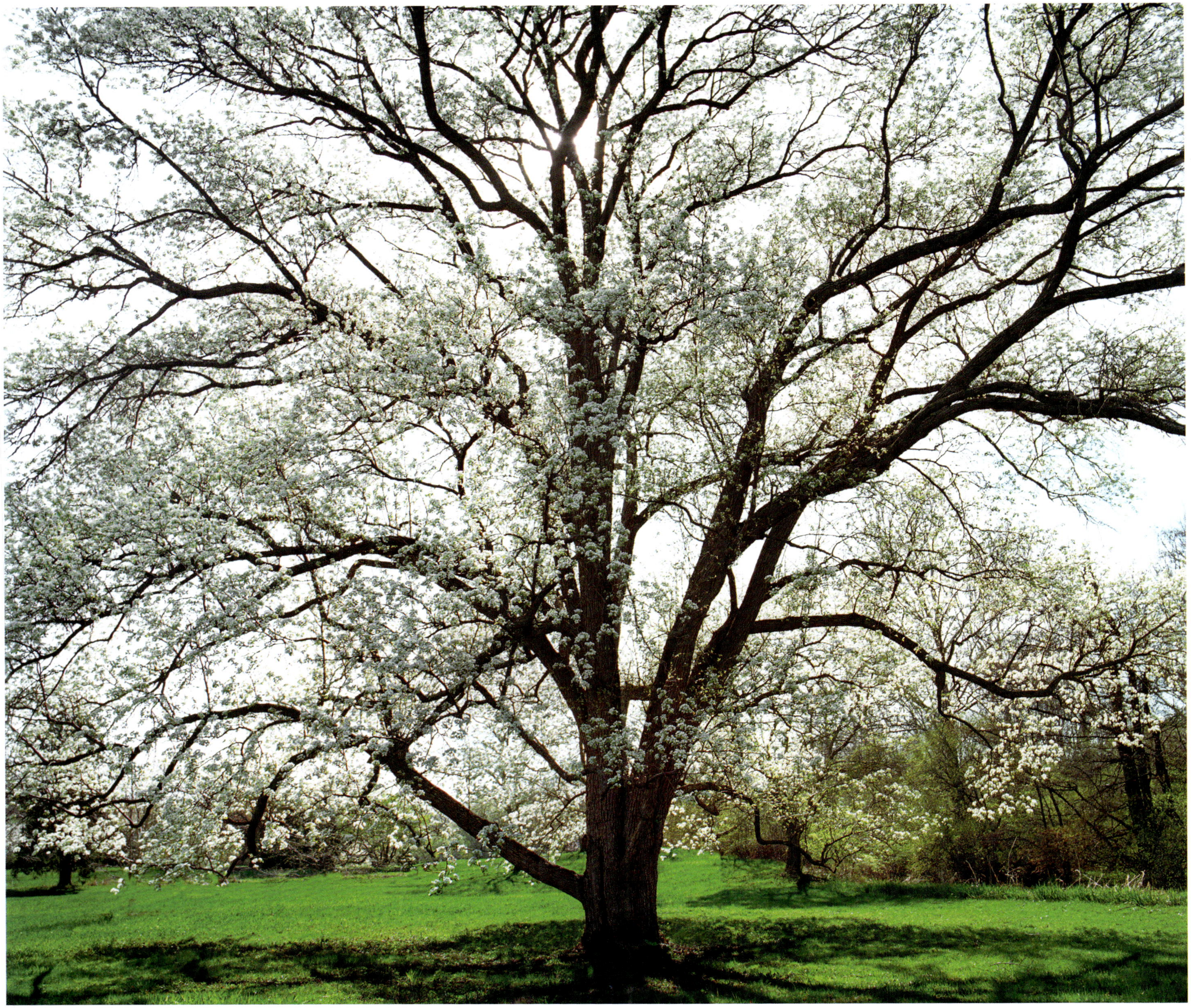

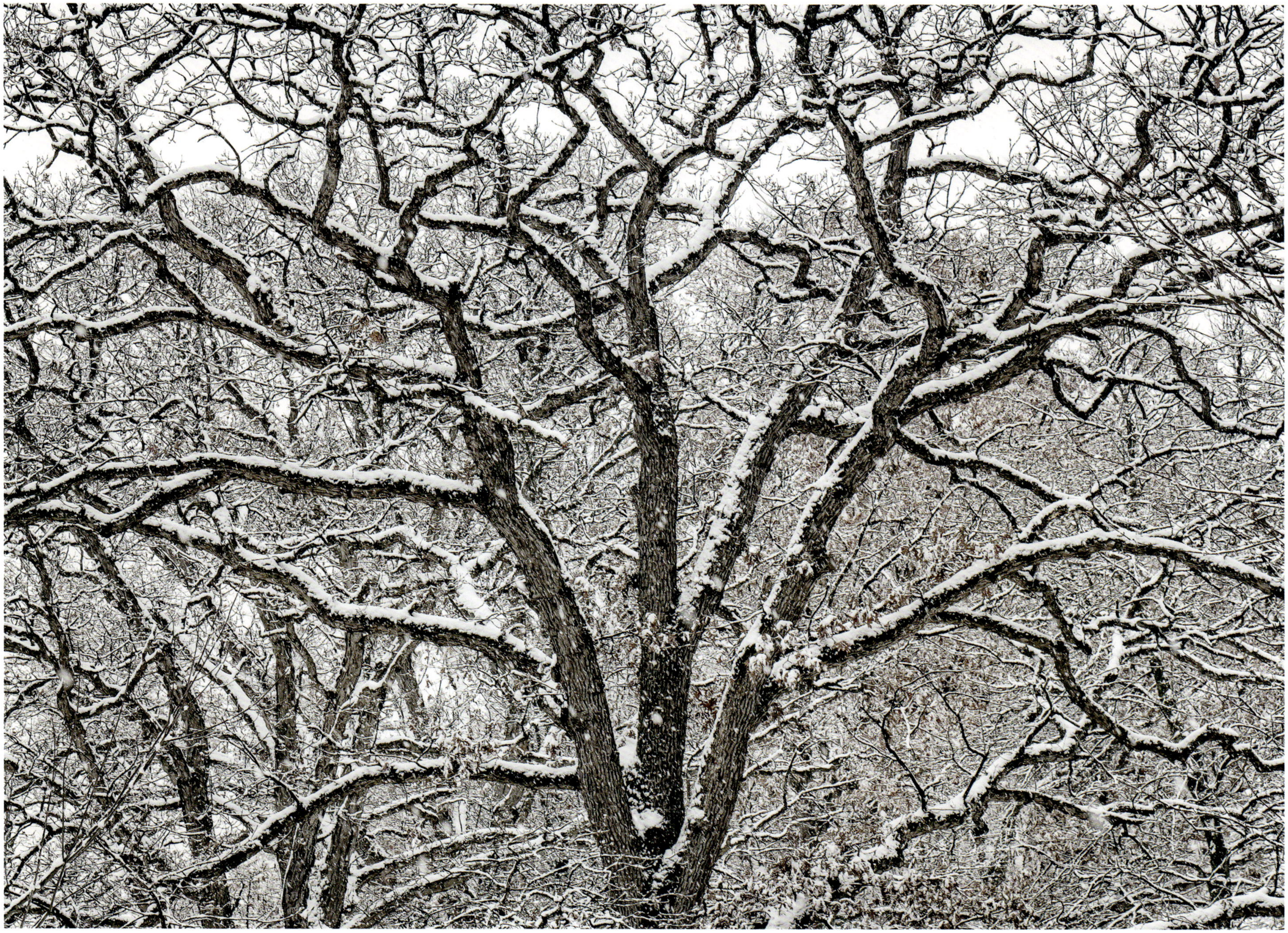

82. *Flowering Pear Tree*, China Collection, near the East Branch, 2005 (opposite)
83. *Snow Covered Oak*, East Side, 2018

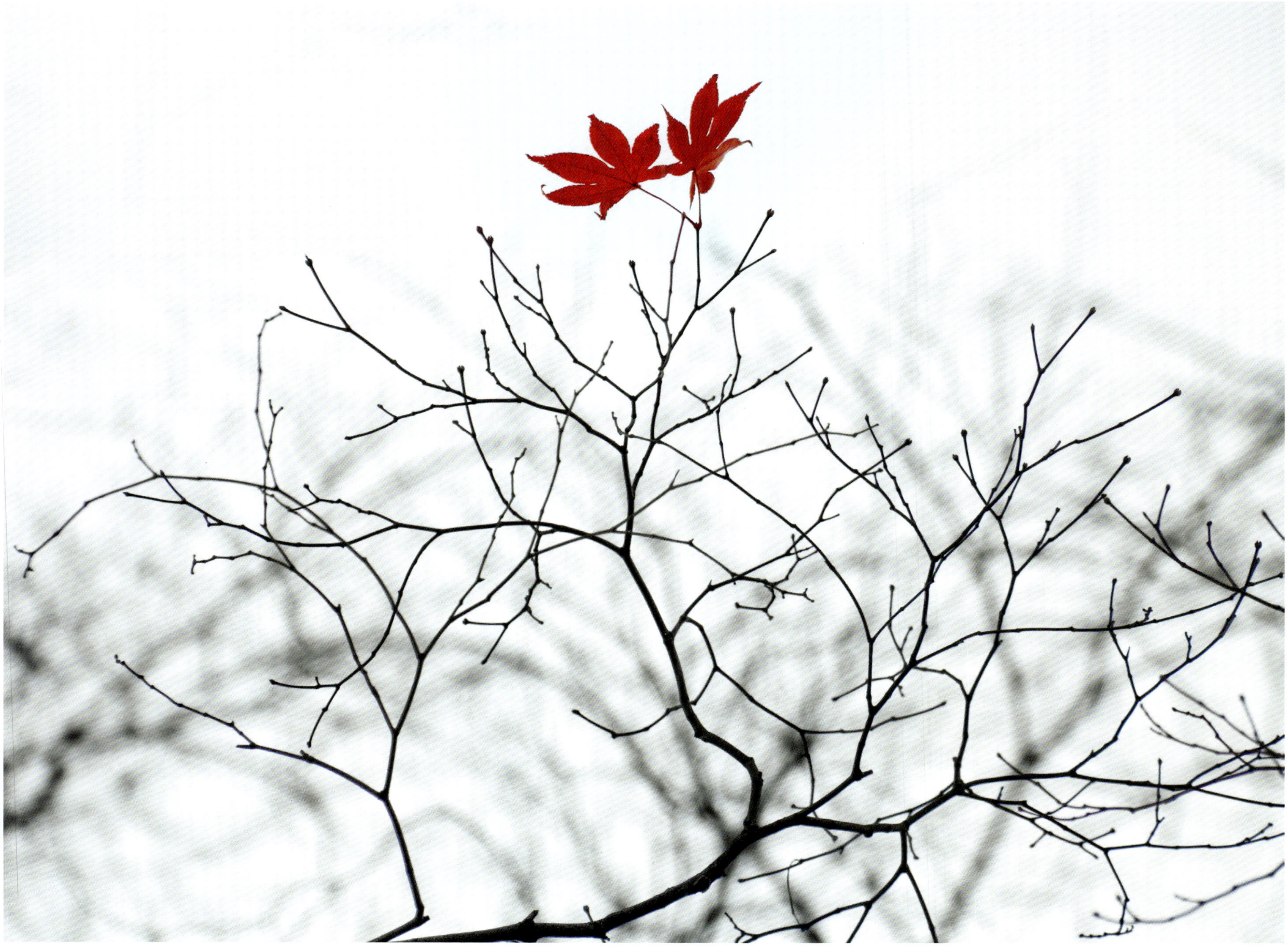

84. *Last Leaves*, Maple Glade, 2009

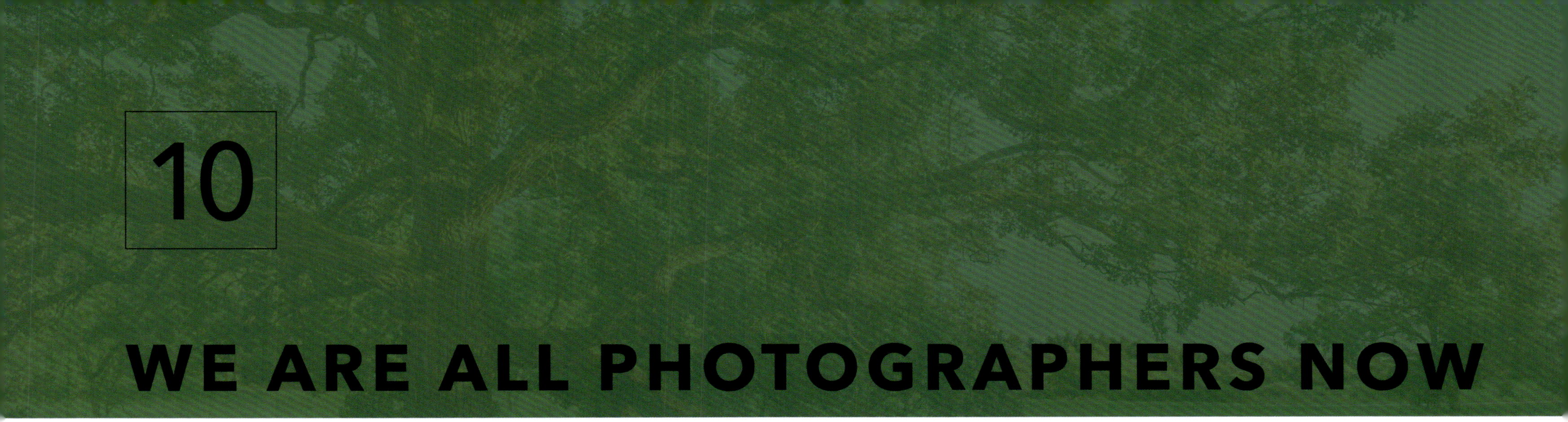

10

WE ARE ALL PHOTOGRAPHERS NOW

The beauty and wonder of nature are available to us, whether we are climbing a mountain, walking in the woods, or simply stopping to consider a blade of grass pushing up through the sidewalk.

Time in nature revives us. We feel recharged whenever we can get outdoors and whenever we can enjoy and contemplate the trees where we live. You can do that at The Morton Arboretum or any forest preserve or green space, whatever is near you, wherever you can easily go to see nature.

There's a difference between taking hundreds of photographs while on a walk and searching for one worthy picture. The first (taking pictures of everything) can interfere with the experience of being there without allowing the experience to have an impact on us. The second can enhance our experience in nature because it encourages us to feel what we're seeing.

Twenty-two years ago, when I started this project, there were just a few of us seeking beautiful and expressive photographs when we came to walk here at The Morton Arboretum. Now nearly every visitor arrives with a smartphone, one with the camera capabilities needed to take technically good photographs.

When going for a walk in the woods, or any kind of nature, bring and use whatever camera or phone with camera capabilities you have. It's not the technology that's taking the picture. It's you; how you feel about what you are seeing at a specific place and time that will make the picture. Experience nature, feel it, distill a bit of the wonder and beauty into worthy pictures of places you go during the time you spend there.

We are all photographers now!

ACKNOWLEDGMENTS

For their special help in making this book possible, I gratefully acknowledge and heartily thank:

Virginia, my wife, for being by my side always, for encouraging me to take photographs and to create this book, for saving some of my now favorite photographs from the bin, for her questions and conversations, which help me see who I am as a photographer, and for her insight and amazing word-smith talent, which helped me say what I want to say in *Light Through the Trees*.

Susanna Chapman, my daughter and brilliant illustrator and book designer, for her valuable criticism and advice on sequencing and pairing the photographs and suggesting refinements to my narrative.

Jeff Masson, Gay Anderson, and Jacque Fucilla, the museum store managers at the Arboretum Store throughout the last twenty-two years, and Kevin Earll, assistant store manager. From 1999 to the present many of the photographs in this book have been continually available for sale in the beautiful and elegant Arboretum Store, thanks to these people. I am deeply grateful to them for selecting my photographs, making them available to the many visitors and members of The Morton Arboretum, connecting my photographs and me to this wonderful audience, and all the while for continually encouraging me to take more photographs at The Morton Arboretum.

I'm deeply grateful to the many talented people at the University of Illinois Press who believed in my book and guided both my book and me through the complex book publication process. In particular, I'm grateful to and give heartfelt thanks to Michael Roux for being more than an excellent marketing manager, which he is, but for also pulling everything together to make this book happen, including the brainstorming that led to the book's beautiful title; Dustin Hubbart, art director, for his overall book design and creative layout and for fine-tuning photographs for best tone and color; Jennifer Argo, assistant managing editor and Mariah Mendes Schaefer, assistant acquisitions editor, for their incisive editing, clarity in suggesting changes, and for guiding me through the intricacies of book publishing. And also, Roberta J. Sparenberg, sales and marketing assistant, for the detailed work she contributed to the marketing process.

It is a moving experience to offer one's creative work to the world, to see the response, and to hear what one's work means to others. I'm grateful to *everyone* who has embraced these photographs that I took (or, as I say in the book, that I "found") at The Morton Arboretum. I mean it when I say, "we are all photographers now." We are, and I look forward to hearing from all and keeping the discussion in this book going at https://www.instagram.com/lightthroughthetrees/ and www.petervagt.com. The path to feeling one's way to finding photographs in nature may be mysterious, but it starts with finding more time to spend in nature and then, of course, bringing a camera with us!

Thank you all!

ABOUT THE PHOTOGRAPHER

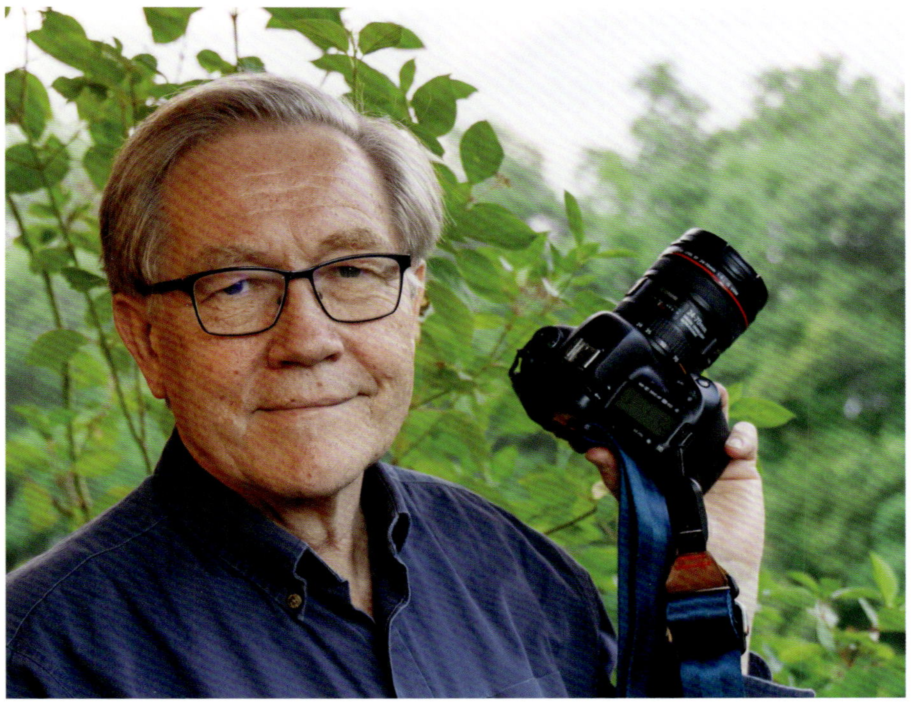

PETER J. VAGT grew up in the farmland of southern Minnesota. From his family's farm, open spaces, a woodland, and a quiet stretch of river were all just a short bike ride away. Choosing a career as an environmental scientist, he came to Chicago for most of his working life. Chicago provided a visual change from Minnesota. Getting to any kind of woodland required biking or driving for miles past endless rows of houses, buildings, busy strip malls, and highways. One day he gratefully discovered The Morton Arboretum, a natural island within an urban landscape, with trails through the woods and paths along a river and brooks. The Arboretum became his favorite place to watch the seasons change and observe nature's dynamic peace.

Over these years, he realized his philosophy of photography. He reaches for what is beyond representation of the subject when taking photographs of stands of trees, intersecting tree branches, reflections of a woodland scene, or simply an individual leaf. He visits the same locations many times throughout each year, waiting for moments of special light, moments that reveal what it feels like, for him, to be at the Arboretum. For him, a successful picture—one that becomes part of his Arboretum Portfolio—does that. These pictures announce what it feels like to be at the Arboretum, what it feels like to see light change as the sun sinks toward the horizon, what a joy it is to watch a mallard glide across a lake, and the quiet presence of two Canada geese communing, surrounded by early morning fog rising from Meadow Lake.

Peter's work is included in many private collections and professional association collections. Since 1999, his Morton Arboretum work has been available to the public at The Arboretum Store. His work has also been exhibited in bookstores, by the Kane County Bar Association, Geneva, Illinois, and at the Forest Preserve District of DuPage County, Wheaton, Illinois. The Arboretum Store exhibited his work as the featured artist in August 2005, November 2006, and October 2007.

The photographs in this book prior to 2005 were taken with Nikon and Hasselblad film cameras. Most photos taken since 2005 were photographed with Canon and Panasonic digital cameras.

The Morton Arboretum, West Side

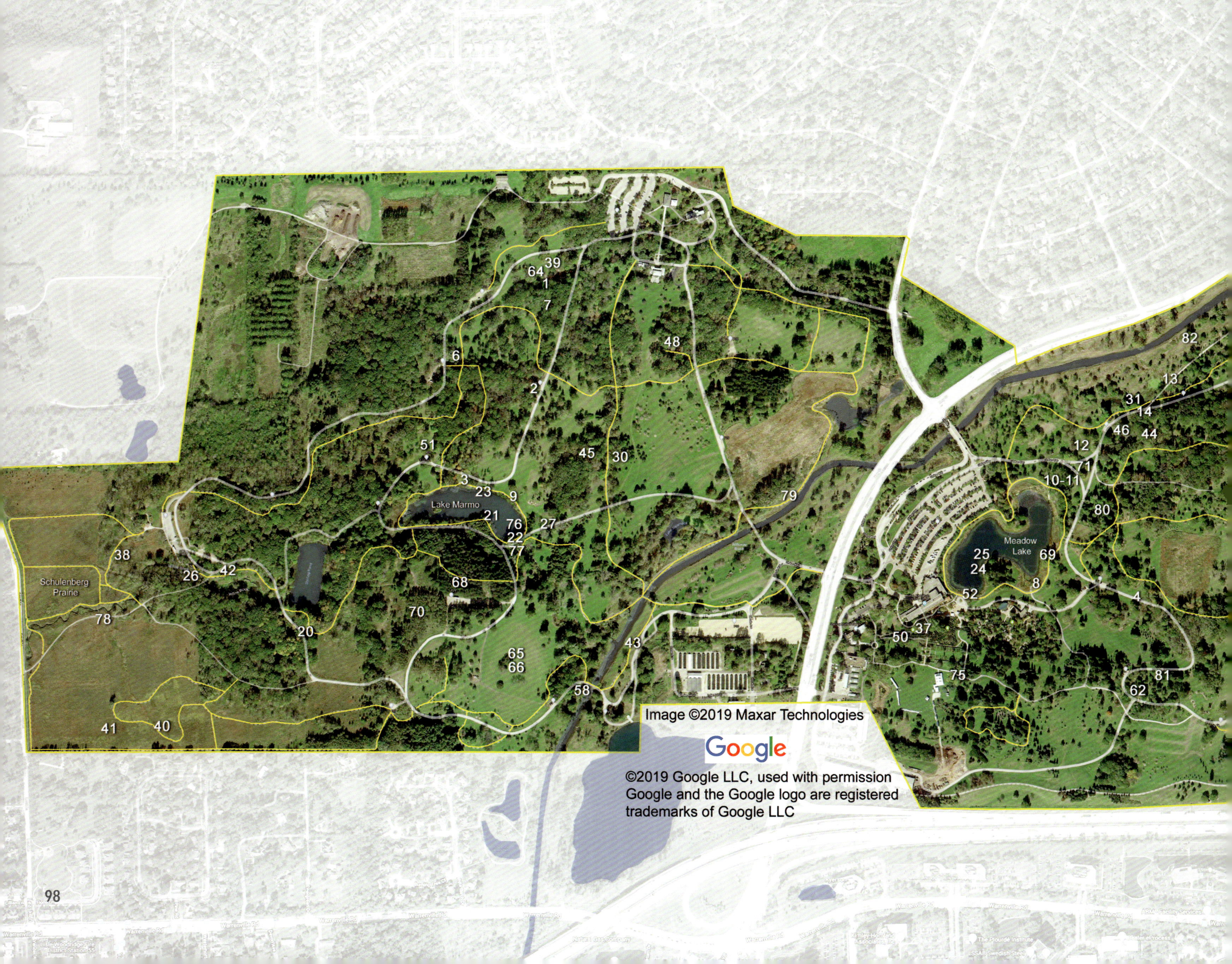

The Morton Arboretum, East Side

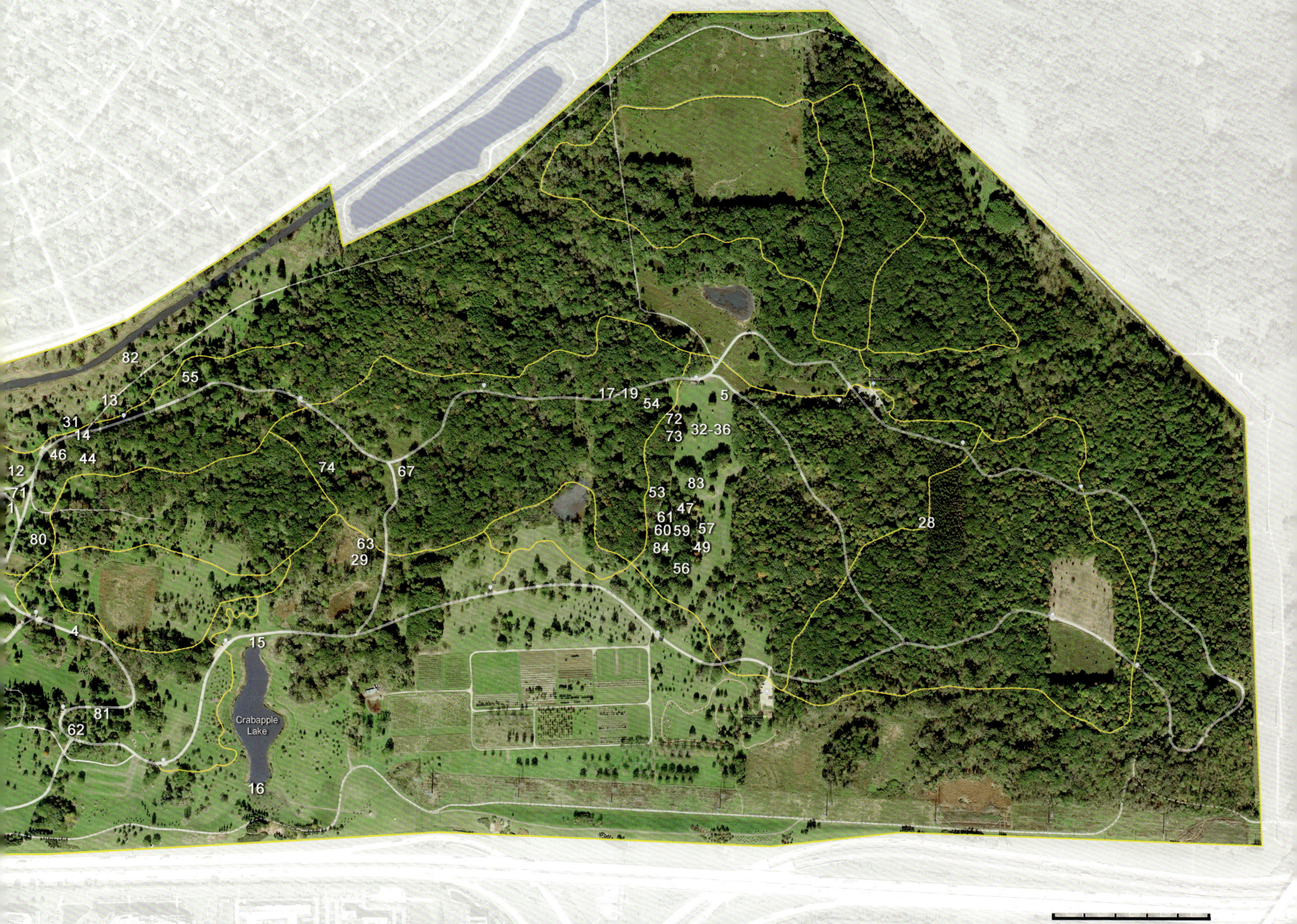

Numbers on this map are the plate numbers of each photograph.
Each plate number shows the location at which the photograph was taken.

The plate number and title of each photograph is also listed on the following page.

LIST OF PHOTOGRAPHS

59. *Japanese Maple Branches*, Maple Glade, November 2002
60. *Japanese Maple Trees*, November 2002
61. *Four Japanese Maples*, Maple Glade, Early November 2005
62. *Japanese Zelkova Leaves*, atop Frost Hill, 2015
63. *Great Oak*, Late November 2014
64. *Lone Runner*, December 2014
65. *Five Chestnut Trees, Bobolink Meadow, November 2017*
66. *Five Chestnut Trees, Bobolink Meadow, January 2015*
67. *Eleven Trees*, East Side, 2007
68. *Spruce Stand*, at Parking Area P29, 2017
69. *April Snow on Meadow Lake*, 2018
70. *Snow Fall on Spruce Hill*, near Parking Area P29, 2017
71. *Cork Tree and Snowflakes at the Intersection*, East Side, 2018
72. *Cut-Leaf European Beech, Late October* 2012
73. *Cut-Leaf European Beech in December Snowfall*, 2001
74. *Snow in the Air, Shadows on the Snow*, 2004
75. *Cork Tree in New Snow*, near the Hedge Collection, 2008
76. *Leaves on Frozen Lake Marmo*, 2017
77. *Floating Leaves*, below Bridge at Rainbow Falls, 2012
78. *Spent Grass*, Schulenberg Prairie, 2018
79. *Willoway Flourish*, 2019
80. *Bent Pine*, near the Eastside Trailhead, 2009
81. *Pines atop Frost Hill*, East Side, 2013
82. *Flowering Pear Tree*, China Collection, near the East Branch, 2005
83. *Snow Covered Oak*, East Side, 2018
84. *Last Leaves*, Maple Glade, 2009

The University of Illinois Press
is a founding member of the
Association of University Presses.

Text designed by Dustin J. Hubbart
Composed in Avenir Next 10/15
with Avenir Next Bold display
by Dustin J. Hubbart
at the University of Illinois Press
Printed in China through Martin Book Management

University of Illinois Press
1325 South Oak Street
Champaign, IL 61820-6903
www.press.uillinois.edu